Dreaming Realities

A Spiritual System To Create Inner Alignment Through Dreams

by

Julie Silverthorn M.S.
&
John Overdurf C.A.C.

Crown House Publishing Limited

First published in the UK by

Crown House Publishing Limited
Crown Buildings
Bancyfelin
Carmarthen SA33 5ND
Wales
UK

First published 1999

British Library of Cataloguing-in-Publication Data
A catalogue entry for this book is available
from the British Library.

ISBN 1899836306

Printed and bound in Wales by
WBC Book Manufacturers
Waterton Industrial Estate
Bridgend
Wales
UK

Dedication

To the Dream
To the Dreamer
To the One

About the Authors

Julie Silverthorn and John Overdurf are highly respected international therapists and trainers of Hypnotherapy and NLP with over thirty years of combined experience. They are both Certified Master Trainers of NLP and the developers of Humanistic Neuro-Linguistic Psychology™, which integrates hypnosis, neurolinguistics, quantum theory, and spirituality. John is a Certified Addictions Counselor and former instructor of Psychology, while Julie has a Master's Degree in Clinical Psychology.

They are authors of *Training Trances*, an innovative book about the uses of hypnosis in therapy and training. They are currently writing their third book which details their developments of Humanistic Neuro-Linguistic Psychology™. Married to one another for twenty years, they live their dream in the heart of Pennsylvania Dutch Country with their cocker spaniel, Bodhi, and love every minute of it. Right now, they are dreaming realities of sleeping!

Table Of Contents

Acknowledgements

Our deepest thanks and appreciation to all those who supported this dream! ...May your greatest dreams be your only reality!

Special thanks to Harold and Violet James for all their time, energy, expertise, caring, and contributions from our last dream to this one.

Special thanks to Rex and Bobbie Shudde for all their attention and care in helping to refine this dream.

Special thanks to Ed Sisler and David Soehren for their work on the cover and for supporting the project, as good friends do!

Special thanks to Patrice Perillo for so elegantly utilizing and teaching this material.

Special thanks to Alex Roper, David Bowman and everyone at Crown House Publishing for your support. This is a much better dream thanks to you.

Special thanks to all our teachers/friends who have encouraged and shaped our thinking and dreaming over the years: Dr Erickson, Ron Klein, Ardie Flynn, Tad James, Uncle George Naope, and Stephen LaBerge.

Special thanks to Bob Leichtman and ethernet friends for your wisdom, wit, kindness and for modeling how to connect *Heaven and Earth.*

Special thanks to Miles, Trane, Luther and Stevie Ray for their musical companionship and Grace during the editing of this book and our lives in general.

Special thanks to Tempa Uhlrich, our assistant, for all that she has contributed to support our creativity throughout the years she has worked with us. You're a gift!

Special thanks to our parents: Tony & Jeanne Overdurf, and Ivan & Agnes Silverthorn for always believing in our dreams.

Special thanks to our dear companions in this dreaming reality, Rio and Bodhi.

Special thanks to Sai Baba for his love and guidance, and especially for transcending time and space by visiting us in our dreams. And...thanks for ALL THAT IS.

Introduction

Dreaming is something that comes naturally to all of us. We do it every night and it is as automatic as the sleep that surrounds it. Sometimes we even dream during the day. We dream unconsciously; we do not have to plan to do it, although when we do pay attention to our dreams, we change them. It is a lot like other unconscious processes that we may take for granted. Think of all the processes that our unconscious regulates for us automatically: respiration, digestion, sensation, perception, memory storage, endocrine and immunological functions, motor skills and many others. It seems that, as human beings, the things that are of utmost importance to us are, by necessity, automatic or unconscious. Why? Think what would happen if we ever forgot to do one of them for any period of time. What if we forgot to digest our food or became so preoccupied with something that we forgot to breathe? While reading this book you might want to consider, "Why would a greater intelligence than us bother to include ***dreaming*** as one of these ***automatic*** unconscious processes? What purpose does dreaming have?"

Dreams demonstrate the power of the unconscious. Most of us have been emotionally moved by the power of a dream at some point in our lives. We wake up and lie motionless in that half-awake, half-asleep state. The feelings seem so "real." Yet, at other times, dreams seem completely nonsensical. They do not seem "real" at all; if anything, they seem more surreal, like a movie made from the out-takes of everyday life errantly spliced together by some eccentric "art movie" director. Come to think of it, who *is* the director, anyway? Despite all the nonsense, few people go through this life without wondering about dreams and their meanings. We have all had the experience of awakening from a dream, feeling profoundly affected, and thinking, "There must be something to this." Then we get up, get on with our day and only later do we think, "What was that dream all about?" It seemed important at the time. Even if we did not remember the dream, the power of its memory still remained. We experienced it and it affected us—perhaps in the same way that things from long ago had a profound effect on our lives, even though they were completely outside our conscious awareness and long since forgotten.

Dreams are hypnotic. They suck us in. Each night when we dream we visit our own self-generated, internal reality. It is a narrative, running parallel to our conscious, waking life. In our dreams we see, hear, feel, think—and, in some cases, taste and smell—just as we do when we are awake. We carry on relationships, meet new people, often go to school, work, travel, make love and all the other kinds of things that make up what we call life. Sometimes we even dream in a dream!

In our dreams we are very much alive. Dreams can be so convincing at the time that we do not even question if we are dreaming. We just get swept away with our own story line. (We ought to know what would do it!) We adapt to sudden changes that may be contradictory, inconsistent, threatening, or surreal, in the time it takes to think a new thought. The usual constructs of time and space are stretched, twisted, inverted, juxtaposed; however it happens, they are gone!

We can be talking to a childhood friend whom we have not seen for years, in our old neighborhood, and, with the blink of an eye, be on a plane in a different state with people who are unknown but familiar. The next moment, we are in high school and late for a class. Maybe for a second we question, "Haven't I already graduated from high school?" but quickly we are swept away into the reality of the dream. How often do we see the dream reality for what it really is? Often we just accept it as it is on the surface; just like a positive hypnotic suggestion given in trance; just like the everyday trances and dreams that we accept without question in our "waking" state about who we are, why we are here and what is possible. Do we get the messages from these dreams? Do we use our dreams for guidance and transcend their realities or do we get swept away in the drama of our own narrative?

Dreams can change our life. It is just a matter of whether we have any say in it or not. One incredible resource we have when we dream is the ability to explore possibilities and realities that are beyond what we could do in the physical world. We are freed from the limitations of our everyday sense of logic, time, space, and order. We can use our night dreams to support or change our waking reality and vice versa. As we will discuss later in more detail, "our dreamer" (our unconscious and Higher Self) is our own private therapist who works the nightshift, doing several sessions every night—solving problems, enhancing creativity, beginning new projects, and finding meaning in life. However, as in the case of most professionals, some payment is expected to ensure we have invested in the process. In this life you have to pay, and with *this* therapist you pay with your attention.

We are all dreaming realities and living dreams. We do this whether we are awake or asleep. We do it whether it is night or day. The question is, "Are we living dreams and dreaming realities that matter?" The purpose of this book is to show you how to use your dreams to ***align with your self*** so that the reality you are living matters. We wrote this book as a "how to" book. It is an integration of what we have learned from hypnosis, neuroscience, and dream research, as well as from spiritual systems that emphasize the importance of dreams. We believe that the purpose of most psychological and spiritual systems is to produce alignment among the conscious, unconscious, and higher conscious minds. If you are wondering what we mean by this, then you will learn something new in these pages. If you understand this notion of alignment, then we believe that this book will provide you with a deeper understanding and appreciation of **how** you can use your dreams to create alignment inside your self.

The processes in this book have been modified or developed over the years for optimal results. You may find that even the casual use of these approaches can add to your life. These approaches have certainly added to ours. Some of them require a fair amount of commitment on your part, but the results will be worth that commitment. The fact that you are reading this book is an indication that you are interested in dreams and ***want to learn more***. It is no mistake that you are reading this book. How far you go with these practices is up to you. Our job is to suggest ***possibilities***. One of these possibilities may be that the dream material is not for you. If so, then you have ***learned something important for yourself*** and you can direct your efforts toward another dream that is worth living.

This book just happens to be one dream that an intelligence far greater than ours wanted us to write. And as we have spent a fair amount of time exploring all of this, we can say that it has added depth to our lives for which we are very grateful.

Julie Silverthorn and John Overdurf
March 1999
Lancaster, PA, USA

Tips For Getting The Most From **Dreaming Realities**

Welcome to ***Dreaming Realities***. Before you continue, here are a few tips we would like to offer you to make your reading more enjoyable and your time more productive. You might notice, in perusing this book, that it is divided into seven chapters and seven *Dreamtime Interludes*. Together they form an integrated dream system whose purpose is to align your conscious, unconscious, and higher conscious minds.

The first three chapters explore the three minds, the physiology of sleep, and the quantum physics of dreaming. They integrate the most important and up-to-date information that we have found about dreams and related states. These chapters form the content basis of the dreaming practices covered in the last four chapters. At the end of each of the chapters we include a conscious review and an unconscious review. The conscious reviews succinctly cover the high points and the important facts that are germane to the dreaming practices taught in the later chapters.

The unconscious reviews, on the other hand, are written to stimulate more general associations and to connect the themes at the unconscious level. Also, they are designed to offer suggestions that can incubate between reading the chapters and other readings. They contain hypnotic language useful in formatting the unconscious mind for exercises in the later chapters and the Dreamtime Interludes. You may find it useful to read these reviews repeatedly as you continue with the later chapters.

The middle and later chapters cover dream incubation, interpretation, lucidity, and advanced spiritual practices using sleep and dreams. These chapters are less content-oriented and are more "how to." Generally, it is preferable that you carry out the processes in the order presented, because they are progressive.

The end of the book includes seven Dreamtime Interludes. Each interlude is a process, or series of processes, that can greatly enhance the techniques found in the first seven chapters. The first interlude is a reality-testing procedure that will sharpen your conscious abilities—a crucial step to dreaming lucidly. This process has been researched by a number of prominent lucid dreaming researchers and we can reassure you that it works. We have modified these steps to make reality-testing more effective.

The second, third, and fourth interludes will assist you in getting to know your unconscious mind. Two of these interludes will teach you how to use a pendulum to conduct an unconscious review of abilities, memories, beliefs, behaviors, and other resources which can be activated to accelerate your progress. The latter interlude is an unconscious clearing and healing technique that can be used for issues, blocks, or challenges that may arise along the path. It can also be used in conjunction with interpretation to resolve issues that may emerge.

The fifth interlude is a meditation to access your higher conscious mind. We developed the meditation from the work of Roberto Assagioli, the originator of Psychosynthesis, one of the first credible treatment modalities recognizing the higher conscious mind.

The sixth interlude is what we call the Dreaming Meditation Technique. It is a technique we developed after studying and identifying commonalities in numerous dream yoga and meditation systems. For best results, begin using this meditation before chapter 4 on incubation. As you will learn while reading the book, reality-testing and Dreaming Meditation complement each other. They define and then unite the waking state with the dreaming state. Together they form the foundation for the practice of lucid dreaming.

The final interlude is Moe Uhane, the Hawaiian Dreamtime Chant which was translated from Hawaiian by our friends, Tad James and Ardie Flynn.

Chapter 1

Dreaming Our Selves, Each With A Mind Of Its Own

Dreams are metaphors. Our dreams are metaphors of creation. We take something from nothing and create endless possibilities. We can be anyone we want in our dreams, in any place we want. Our dreams provide a nightly refuge from the "sanity" of a linear, predictable world. The "insanity" of dreams provides a cathartic balance for living life in a Newtonian world. In our dreams we can fly. In our waking life we cannot. These are equal, but separate, realities. One is as real as the other and both provide balance in our lives. Just as night follows day, unpredictability follows predictability. Exploring the world of unpredictability creates unlimited possibilities for all that is predictable, in the same way that eventually day follows night.

What Is The Purpose Of Dream Practices?

Achieving alignment is the primary purpose for developing dream practices. The goal is to have as full and as complete an alignment as possible among the conscious, unconscious, and higher conscious minds. Each mind has an equally important role to play. Alignment occurs when all three minds cooperate harmoniously in fulfilling these roles. When they are aligned, integration occurs within the individual. These are the moments, or periods, in life where everything unfolds easily and effortlessly. Things simply go well. We feel good, we are inspired, our relationships go smoothly, and overall we simply enjoy life.

In this state of alignment direct communication occurs among the conscious, unconscious, and higher conscious minds. Information flows easily and naturally among them. Unfortunately, most people do not experience this type of alignment on a consistent basis. Inner conflict is something that many people experience.

When it occurs, it means there is some type of conflict among the conscious, unconscious, and higher conscious minds. The communication channels are either non-existent or blocked, causing turmoil and conflict. Trauma (physical or emotional pain) is usually the precursor to these blockages. When people are traumatized it is still possible for them to receive information. However, they may override this information because they no longer trust their ability to differentiate between what causes pain and what produces alignment.

When we experience alignment, unlimited possibilities exist. Our relationships and our personal issues, as well as our inner and outer healing and our ability to be creative, may all be enhanced by our dreamlife—if we choose to use this source! Life itself is a process of learning; dreams are simply one of the palettes from which we create our reality. Our dreamlife provides an infinite landscape of possibilities for any issue with which we are dealing; all we have to do is choose to use it.

This "dream" is about the ways which are available for promoting alignment. Ultimately, the first step in creating alignment is the willingness to realize that **no matter what you think you are you are always more than that**! Your conscious mind cannot ever fully conceive of the totality of who you really are. The sooner you realize that you are so much more than you think you are (and capable of so much more than you think), the easier your life will become. After recognizing this, it is then a matter of being willing to ask your conscious, unconscious, and higher conscious minds for assistance. Alignment begins with communication between the conscious and the unconscious minds. Why? Because the role of the conscious mind is to initiate the process and the job of the unconscious mind is to carry it out—by being the conduit for information between the higher conscious mind and the conscious mind. We believe that **all problems result from a lack of rapport and alignment among the three minds**. Therefore, all of the techniques in our system are designed to promote the free flow of communication and inner alignment. Now what is important is the recognition of how our conscious, unconscious, and higher conscious minds function and work together to make living and dreaming a series of deeply enriching experiences.

The Three Minds

One of the basic presuppositions of our dream system is that we all have "three minds," also referred to in other systems as the "three selves." We all have a conscious mind, an unconscious mind, and a higher conscious mind. The term "three minds" is actually a reference to the fact that the mind has **three separate functions**. Each of these minds has a particular role in regard to dreaming. If you want a more in-depth discussion of the conscious and unconscious minds, please refer to our book *Training Trances.*

Illustration Of The Three Minds

Higher Conscious Mind
"Guide"

Conscious Mind
"Director"

Unconscious Mind
"Symbol Maker"/"Arena"

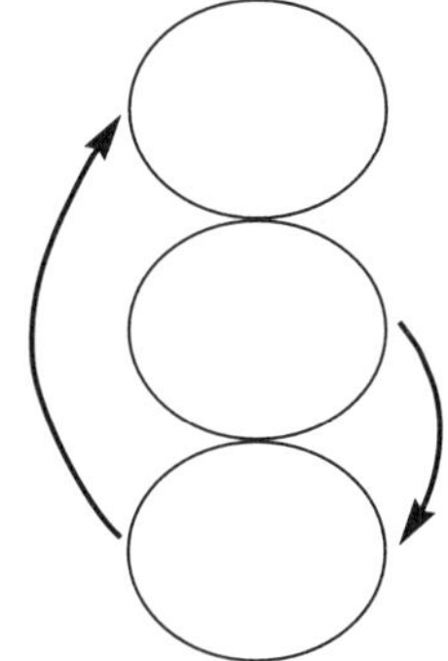

Initially information flows from the unconscious mind to the higher conscious mind, and not from the conscious mind to the higher conscious mind. This means that we cannot rely solely upon our intellect to communicate or connect with our Higher Self. The response from the higher conscious mind then occurs in a downward direction passing through both the conscious and unconscious minds. An example of this would be an intuition accompanied by a tingling feeling and the awareness of both. When the three minds are aligned, as above, it is easy to see that from the position of the higher conscious mind, when looking down, they appear as only one mind. In this instance, the connection to the higher conscious mind is no longer relevant because its boundaries as a separate entity cease to exist. In this state "flow" and harmony abound.

The Conscious Mind

We define the conscious mind as our "**current awareness**" or the focus of our present attention. It represents only a relatively small band of information compared to all the information which is available. It is limited in scope to its own awareness and, if its awareness expands beyond a certain point, it can no longer process incoming information. As a laser beam in a darkened room does not illuminate the entire room, the conscious mind only illuminates the area where its concentration is focused. All of that which remains dark is beyond its immediate scope. Psychologists have determined that the scope of the conscious mind is limited to 7±2 pieces of simultaneous information. This means that when more than five to nine pieces of information are received, the conscious mind becomes overwhelmed and can no longer pay attention to incoming information. You have probably experienced this when you have been very busy. Perhaps people are talking, phones are ringing, the kids are crying, you are trying to get something done, and all of a sudden there is so much going on that you cannot stand it. You have just discovered the limits of your conscious mind!

The conscious mind corresponds approximately to what scientists identify as "dominant-hemisphere functioning." This means that the conscious mind corresponds to the brain hemisphere which is dominant for a particular individual—a right-handed person would be left-hemisphere dominant and a left-handed person would be right-hemisphere dominant. While this metaphor of hemispheric dominance is overly simplified and therefore not completely accurate, it does provide a good working understanding of the conscious mind's functioning. It is safe to say that the conscious mind is logical, linear, sequential, analytical, deductive, rational, and language oriented. It is also our intellect.

Many spiritual practices advocate increasing conscious awareness in the process of personal evolution. Because our band of awareness in the journey through life is often so limited, it is important to expand awareness as much as possible. When we are "mindful" in all of our actions, decisions, and choices, alignment increases as communication flows more fully among the three minds.

The Unconscious Mind

If the conscious mind is our present awareness, then the unconscious mind is **everything else**. It is all of the darkened areas in the room where the laser beam does not shine. In contrast to the conscious mind, the unconscious can process millions of pieces of information simultaneously without becoming overwhelmed. Because of this the unconscious mind is responsible for everything we do automatically. Learning, healing, walking, driving a car, metabolizing our food, and countless other processes which happen automatically are all carried out by the unconscious mind. In the metaphor of hemispheric dominance the unconscious mind corresponds approximately to the subdominant hemisphere. The unconscious mind for a right-handed person would be equivalent to the right hemisphere and for a left-handed person it would be the left hemisphere. It is intuitive, artistic, holistic, simultaneous, non-linear, and inductive. The unconscious is known as the "storehouse" because our memories and our emotions are stored there. Our unconscious mind is also our body. It is responsible for all of the complex biochemical processes which occur on both micro and macro levels. Additionally, it is the repository for our beliefs about our identity, the world around us, and what we believe is possible.

Because the unconscious mind stores our beliefs and emotions it will tend to be true to what it has learned over the years, rightly or wrongly. Its intentions are always adaptive. It wants to do the best it can with the choices available. Sometimes the choices may not seem to be the best ones, especially if they are clouded with negative emotions. Fear, anger, pain, hurt, sadness, anxiety and/or other uncomfortable emotions can influence the functioning of the unconscious mind. And, as situations change, beliefs that were once adaptive may now be limiting and even dysfunctional. These beliefs can even pertain directly to dreams and affect how well we remember them, how much we value them, and how well we utilize them in our personal evolution.

The Higher Conscious Mind

The "Higher Self," or the higher conscious mind, is our "guide." It is the part of us that has access to the archetypes which Jung referred to in his concept of the "collective unconscious"...and it is more than that! The higher conscious mind is our **direct connection** with the Infinite, the Universe, the Divine, or God. The Higher Self is our connection to the intelligence and information that comprises the whole of the Universe and beyond. In dualistic terms, our Higher Self is our connection to Spirit. In synergistic terms our Higher Self **is** spirit. It has access to all the information that is, because it **is** that information.

The higher conscious mind also represents perfection, as we might conceptualize it with our limited conscious mind understanding. To the Higher Self everything is as it should be. There is no judgement at this level because everything is okay as it is. This is in contrast to the unconscious mind which may operate judgementally based upon its emotions and beliefs. At the moment when we are aligned with our higher conscious mind we are the closest experientially to understanding grace while in the physical form. Through our Higher Self we come to know God, the Divine, and the Universe (or whatever labels we choose to use).

The Role Of The Three Minds In Dreaming

Our belief is that all dreams are messages from the higher conscious mind. Our Higher Self wants to guide us in all we do. It communicates to us in various ways—through certain events, through our relationships with others, and through our intuition. However, because of our "free will", it generally does so in a non-intrusive way. As a higher form of life we are always at choice—we have the freedom to say "yes," or "no," and to choose right from wrong. The higher conscious mind will not interfere with our choices, because from the position of the Higher Self all is as it should be. The only times when it may intervene directly are in life-and-death circumstances. You have probably heard of people who had a sense that something was not right, so they did not take the flight on which they were scheduled. Or perhaps through a series of events, they missed their flight and were better off because they had. These are examples of how the Higher Self intervenes and guides our lives.

Our dreams are examples of how the Higher Self intervenes non-intrusively to guide us. We have the freedom to pay attention to our dreams or not. If we pay attention a message will always be there. The message will be sent to help us, and may affirm what we are already doing or provide us with insight into other choices of which we were not aware. Therefore, one of the primary results of dreaming is connection with the Higher Self to produce greater alignment in our lives.

How does this actually occur? The entire process begins with the conscious mind. Its primary function is to be the "director." It determines what to do and when to do it. In terms of dreaming, the conscious mind is aware of the choices for dreamtime practices. It is responsible for making or not making these choices, and for following up afterwards to determine the results. Dreamtime practices begin and end with the conscious mind. It chooses whether to incubate a dream, to have a lucid dream, and whether to interpret or analyze afterward. As the "director" it provides "direction" for which processes will occur. Because our conscious mind so actively runs the show during the day, each night when we sleep it is really our conscious mind that sleeps. It takes a break as the unconscious processes take center stage. If the conscious mind wants to participate more fully in dreamtime practices it can develop its awareness while sleeping. A lucid dream occurs when we wake up in a dream and realize we are dreaming while we are still asleep. If the conscious mind chooses to play in this way, it will add to the alignment among the three minds.

The primary role of the unconscious mind in dreaming is to provide the **arena** for the dreams. It is the theater where the information is played out. In this theater there is a multitude of scheduled performances occurring on many different levels—biochemical, emotional, psychological, and spiritual. Some of these performances are memorable, some are not. For example, it is not important for us to remember consciously that our nervous system is stocking up on neuropeptides and that healing occurs while we sleep. These processes occur automatically outside our awareness while we rest and are entertained.

Within this theater or arena, the unconscious mind also provides the **language** for dreams. That language is in the form of symbols. Each person's unconscious mind creates symbols which are unique. It develops these symbols from associations, experiences, and memories. Our life experiences become the building blocks for our personal dream symbology. Because these symbols are created from personal experience, we believe that "stock interpretations" are not as valid as individual interpretations. Rather, these symbols represent the message from **our** higher conscious mind.

For the message from the higher conscious mind to reach us it must come through the unconscious mind. Therefore, the unconscious mind holds the keys. It is the dream weaver in the sense that it weaves the message of the higher conscious mind into our personal symbology. The unconscious mind codes the messages and puts them in a form that is acceptable and palatable to the conscious mind. This also means that some information may not be available to the conscious mind until it is ready for that information, or it makes a request, or life's circumstances require it. If we imagine for a moment looking at things from the point of view of the Higher Self, we understand that **everything is as it ought to be**. Therefore, the Higher Self has no insistence that the conscious mind heed its messages and guidance. Why should it? It has access to the "big picture." It knows everything is working as it should. The problem is that most of us either do not know this experientially or believe it only from moment to moment. In fact, we might say that this is one reason we are alive: to realize, in physical form, that everything is as it should be!

Once the conscious mind sets the direction it lets things unfold unconsciously. Essentially our conscious mind is the last to know what is happening in the process. We wake up in the morning and perhaps we remember some of what we dreamed. The conscious mind can choose to consider those dreams and even interpret them if it wants. **Remember, ultimately, the conscious mind is**

free to accept or deny anything that is occurring at the unconscious or higher conscious levels. That is the beauty of our existence. We have the free will to pay attention and make meaning in our own way, in our own time. The more the conscious mind pays attention to the dream and intelligently uses this communication, the more the rapport and alignment among the three minds will increase.

For example, have you ever had a dream where you woke up in the morning, did not remember much about the dream but immediately understood its meaning? In this case, we would say that the message from the higher conscious mind was presented in a fairly direct way by the unconscious mind and it became immediately available to the conscious mind. In other words, the higher conscious mind, in its own wisdom said, "Well, she is really ready for this one. We do not need to dress it up to make it more acceptable to her; we will just say it the way it is!" One litmus test of how prepared we are to deal with the truth is how consistently we put the messages into action.

This system has inherent checks and balances, depending on our actions. Do we really follow through on the messages? If we do not take action, our unconscious mind and our higher conscious mind know that we are not paying attention and listening to them. In this case they will continue sending stronger and stronger messages until we ask, "Why does this issue keep coming up for me?" Once we listen to the message, we become an active participant in our dreamlife. This is one surefire way to establish **deeper and deeper rapport and alignment with the three minds**, because they know that each of their roles is being respected. If we accept the presupposition that the higher conscious mind is communicating these messages to us in the form of dreams, why would we not want to be open to these messages? If we are open to such messages, then, in dream practices, as in hypnosis, we are deepening the rapport among our conscious, unconscious, and higher conscious minds. When we do this, we are in the flow of life. Events seem to occur easily and spontaneously...and the more we listen to our dream messages, the more our lives will continue to unfold easily and spontaneously—as will the next part of this dream.

Conscious Review Of Chapter 1

1. **A dream is a reality that we have created**. A dream can come in the form of night dreams, daydreams, beliefs, and trances. Even our waking life can be a dream.

2. **We are always living dreams and dreaming realities**. The purpose of living dreams and dreaming realities is to produce alignment among the conscious, unconscious, and higher conscious minds.

3. **The conscious mind's purpose is to be aware and to be present**. It is excellent at analyzing information and making discriminations. It is constantly orienting us to what is "real" in the world.

4. **The unconscious mind runs all of our automatic functions**. It communicates through sensations, thoughts, and internal images. Its language is symbols. It knows how to heal the body and consolidate learning. It processes data simultaneously on multiple levels.

5. **The higher conscious mind or Higher Self is who we really are**. It is our connection to God and our guide through this life. It provides moments of inspiration that stay for life. It is always there. If it is asked, it will speak through life itself.

6. **Alignment is built on acceptance, rapport, and communication within**. When we are aligned we know it. We are living through our Higher Self and we flow with life.

Unconscious Review Of Chapter 1

You all know that you have a conscious mind and that you have an unconscious mind...and perhaps you now know you have a higher conscious mind. As you are reading this, it is your conscious mind that has directed you to this spot. You have an intention to read this and so you do, because your unconscious mind is automatically focusing your eyes and secreting chemicals that activate the optic nerve...relaying information through your thalamus which in turn relays impulses that activate certain neural networks throughout your cortex and limbic system...finally resulting in the visual representation that comes together with the activation of your occipital lobe, and you see what you have been seeing now!

And you do not have to know any of this consciously. All you do is intend something and to the extent that ***you have rapport*** with your unconscious mind, it does the rest for you automatically. While you are reading these words, without your knowledge, your unconscious mind is...connecting to the information that is most important to you. We do not know what those connections are, but we do know that your unconscious will...***be guided by your higher conscious mind***...to make those connections...that will serve you and you are continuing learning, growth, and ***healing***. After all that is its purpose...to guide you. All you have to do is ***pay attention*** consciously.

You may find that at the end of each chapter of this book we will be communicating to you in a different way than we had previously. This is to help prepare you for the techniques presented later in the book.

Perhaps you will notice the syntax, punctuation, and the type of language that we use may...***be different***. ***You***...might wonder why or you may already know at some level—because you are reading this book for a reason. In fact, it may be for many reasons that you do not know yet but may learn as you read on. There have been lots of times in your life when you began something for a specific reason...perhaps you might want to let your mind wander about that...when you began to ***learn***...learning something for a specific reason...that was ***important for you*** because it had far-reaching effects in your life...as you now know it...in these types of situations you do not know what all the reasons are for why...you are doing this. In fact, you would have know way of knowing what you are ***learning unconsciously*** by reading this. You could not, because it is your unconscious...that is learning now.

There are many things that you know and many things that you do not know. Much of what you learned in life you do not know consciously, but you can use it through your ***intention***. You really do not know consciously how you learned to ***dream,*** but you know how to do it. You do not really know consciously how you learned to sleep, but you do it. You ***intend*** it...let go...and it happens automatically...just as automatically as your eyes are moving across this page, that you can now feel happening...just as certainly as you are...living...this...dream...at this moment...in your life...and all of the moments you have lived...all of the moments...you will ***live***...and ***dream***...the one you are here to do...the one you are here to live...as the universe's only expression of this person who is reading this... You are... Now...!

In a moment you might even feel like **putting this book down** and **closing your eyes**. Not because we have just suggested it but because it would feel comfortable to do so. It gives your unconscious mind time to consolidate what **you have learned** so far in a way that is meaningful to you. It gives your conscious mind, and your eyes, time **to rest** so they can focus intently later on...

Chapter 2

Sleep:
The Chemistry Between The Mechanics And Their Dreams

In this part of the dream, we are going to explore the physiological, psychological, and phenomenological interface between dreams and waking reality. This section is not intended as a definitive source of information on the subject, but rather as the groundwork necessary for dreamtime practices. The basic knowledge of dream physiology will provide a foundation for many of the phenomena and techniques to which we will refer later. We will begin with what "hard science" offers as an understanding of these realities. "Hard science," even with its best explanations, eventually ends up in a dream that is hard to explain without moving beyond the physical...but we are jumping ahead of ourselves! First...

Does Everyone Dream?

Most researchers agree that on the average people have four or five dream periods per night (whenever your "night" may be, in case you actually work at night and sleep during the day). Within each dream period there can be any number of dreams. Many people will be surprised to discover how busy their nightlife really is! Most of us know someone who, when asked about their dreams, says, "I never dream. I sleep like a log and I do not have any dreams at all." The fact of the matter is that everyone dreams to a greater or lesser extent each night when they sleep. Believing that they do not dream or only do so occasionally, is just that, a belief. It is self-hypnosis—beliefs create experience and experience creates beliefs. The bottom line is that the unconscious mind cooperates with whatever waking reality a person has, in order to preserve his/her model of the world.

On the other hand, there are others who remember one or more dreams each night. This is still a small number relative to the total number of dreams we have every night. So why do we not remember more of our dreams? The answer lies in the physiology, or more specifically, the biochemistry of dreams. What is even more interesting is that we can significantly affect our internal biochemistry through psychological means. First, though, we will talk about the physiology of dreams.

Dreams And REM (and we do not mean the band!)

Dreams occur primarily during REM (rapid eye movement) sleep and, at times, during slow-wave (non-REM) sleep. In 1953, at the University of Chicago sleep laboratory, a researcher named Eugene Aserinsky first observed rapid eye movement in children. He found that periods of EEG (brain wave) activation which occurred in sleep were often associated with bursts of rapid eye movement. Intuitively, Aserinsky and his mentor, Nathaniel Kleitman, surmised that rapid eye movement and the accompanying physiological changes in pulse and respiration, were occurring while the subjects were dreaming. To verify this, they began awakening sleeping subjects during the periods of rapid eye movement. When awakened the subjects consistently reported being right in the middle of a dream!

During sleep, motor input is blocked (postural atonia), everywhere **except** the muscles of the eyes. New research now suggests that rapid eye movement (REM) is actually the movement of the eyes relative to what is being seen in the dream and not random movements alone. While opinions differ about this, apparently in a dream the eyes move much as they do in the waking state (Hobson, 1989). For example, if, during REM, a person is watching a car move from left to right, his eyes will move from left to right also.

Ultradian Rhythms

Long before REM sleep was recognized scientists had already discovered **circadian rhythms**. Circadian rhythms, based upon light and dark cycles, function as our internal biological clock. They are reset every 24±0.5 hours to control our internal **daily** rhythms.

Nathaniel Kleitman hypothesized that humans also have internal body rhythms which would have to be shorter in duration than full circadian rhythms (Hobson, 1989). He conducted laboratory studies to observe varying levels of human alertness, arousal, and motor behavior in the waking state. From his research he developed the Basic Rest Activity Cycle (BRAC) study.

The results of the BRAC study led to the discovery of **ultradian rhythms**. Ultradian rhythms refer to the body's basic rest and activity cycles. Each person is active for certain periods of time and then needs to take a rest or a break (coffee breaks, lunchtime, walks, watching TV, etc.). Ultradian rhythms are shorter in duration than circadian rhythms, occurring about sixteen times per day in periods of ninety to one hundred minutes. In addition to this, Kleitman and Aserinsky also recognized that sleep occurred in a ninety to one hundred minute cycle! In fact, they discovered that the BRAC and the sleep cycles were the same.

How Do REM, Sleep, And Hypnosis Compare?

Since the sleep cycle (the ultradian rhythm) continues during the day, so does the REM cycle. The circadian rhythm is the longest cycle, followed by the ultradian rhythm, and the REM cycle is the shortest of the three. REM occurs on a much subtler level during the day than at night. However, the micromuscle movements indicative of REM can be observed as they continue throughout the day. During sleep, these movements become so obvious that researchers can easily observe them in a laboratory environment.

As we mentioned in *Training Trances,* according to Ernest Rossi, Milton Erickson, M.D., the world's foremost expert in hypnotherapy, utilized ultradian rhythms to facilitate trance inductions with his clients. Rossi observed that during a session Erickson often worked with his clients for relatively long periods of time. At one point, Rossi asked Erickson about this and Erickson explained that he would "let things develop" until the client would appear to enter a trance. Rossi believed that Erickson waited until trance developed naturally as a function of the client's ultradian rhythms. (Rossi, 1982)

In our opinion, the only difference between "trancing out" during the day, versus dreaming at night, is that one happens during the day outside of sleep and the other happens at night when physiological sleep is occurring. During the daytime, the rest phase of the ultradian cycle is marked by a generalized shift to parasympathetic arousal (i.e. the relaxation response) and subdominant hemispheric functioning.

Stages Of Sleep: Hypnogogic And Hypnopompic States

In addition, there are other times when we naturally experience trance and dream-like states. These occur immediately before and after sleep. Scientists refer to these as the "hypnogogic" and "hypnopompic" states, respectively. (The easiest way to remember them is in the "hypnogogic" state we "go" to sleep). Most of us are familiar with these stream-of-consciousness states when we are falling off to sleep or when we awaken from sleep. During these times our EEG (brain wave) activity is primarily alpha activity, which parallels both dreaming, trance, and subdominant hemispheric activity. Because of the alpha state these are excellent times for creativity, planning, dream incubation, and dream recall. (Brown, 1991)

i) The hypnogogic state

In the hypnogogic state, we lie down and our bodies start to relax. It is the onset of sleep as we know it. Our brain waves slow down from beta to alpha. We usually have "dreamlets" (i.e. dreamlike stream-of-consciousness images) during this time. We may even incorporate outside stimuli into the dream images and vice versa. Did you ever fall asleep while you were watching a movie and it became part of the dream content? That is common with hypnogogic states. They are dreamlike, but not as intense or as sustained as REM sleep.

While falling asleep, it is common for some people to experience sudden, jerky movements of the body. These movements and twitches occur as the ARAS (the Ascending Reticular Activating System which wakes us up and keeps us alert throughout the day) shuts off voluntary muscle movement. The jerk itself appears to be proportionate to how busy we have been during the day or how much stress we have experienced. It is similar to downshifting a car from sixty miles per hour to zero, as compared to downshifting from twenty-five to zero. Because of this sudden downshifting, sensations of falling are common during hypnogogic sleep.

ii) The hypnopompic state

The hypnopompic state begins as we are aroused from sleep and it generally persists until we begin moving around in bed. The key to staying in this state is to remain still with the eyes closed. This is a very creative state for problem solving and planning the day's activities. This is also the easiest state in which to recall dreams from the previous night. Both the hypnogogic and hypnopompic states are opportune times for practicing dream incubation, positive suggestions, meditation, and healing imagery.

The Sleep Cycle Begins...

As the hypnogogic state ends, the sleep cycle begins. Each sleep cycle is composed of the four stages below, all of which are referred to as non-REM sleep. Technically these are referred to as "descending stages," as we are going into sleep; REM is actually coming out of sleep and is referred to as "ascending." The period of time we spend in each stage varies throughout the night and changes as a function of age. For example, our heaviest sleep usually occurs during the first three hours of sleep—approximately during the first two sleep cycles. This period of non-REM sleep is characterized by extensive Stage IV sleep. Stage IV is the deepest level of sleep with the least activity. This "hibernation" period is necessary for the body to regenerate from daily fatigue and stress. As morning approaches, Stage IV sleep may no longer be as necessary, so Stage III may lead directly to Stage I ascending (REM) sleep.

Table 2.1: EEG Of Non-REM Sleep

Stage (cycles per sec.)	**Frequency** (microvolts)	**Amplitude**	**Wave form**
Stage I	4 - 8	50 - 100	theta waves
Stage II	8 - 15	50 - 150	spindle waves
Stage III	2 - 4	100 - 150	slow waves & spindles
Stage IV	0.5 - 2	100 - 200	delta

(Hobson, 1989)

During Stage IV sleep, primarily delta waves are being emitted. That is when most people are completely gone! What is interesting is that when dream researchers awaken people from delta sleep, which is non-REM or non-dream sleep, they report dreaming. However, these dreams are of a different type from those which occur later in REM sleep. In many cases, these dreams have no mental content whatsoever; they tend to be linear in nature and are usually auditory. The visual component, if present, would be more equivalent to ordinary, waking reality than the bizarre, "outside of time" images which are representative of REM. As the sleep cycle approaches completion, REM, or dream sleep occurs.

Dreaming And The Sleep Cycle

In the **first sleep cycle of the night, dreaming (REM) only occurs for ten minutes toward the very end of the cycle**. (Remember each sleep cycle is ninety to one hundred minutes long.) As sleep progresses, each dream period lengthens, until the final period during which dreaming may comprise ninety percent of the entire sleep cycle. During the last cycle, there is very little, if any, Stage IV sleep. The last cycle is primarily dreaming. Knowing this is very important for dream recall and lucid dreaming practices.

The dreams which occur closest to morning are the ones which we remember best, while the dreams which occur earliest in the evening are the ones we remember least. The first and second cycle are probably the least likely times for lucid dreaming; they have the shortest dream periods with a lot more Stage IV slumber.

Lucid dreaming is much more likely to occur toward morning because the dream cycle has lengthened, thereby increasing the chances of realizing that a dream is occurring.

The Mechanics Of Our REM Realities

During REM, heart rate and blood pressure actually **increase**. Mental activity parallels normal waking activity. The mind is very active while the body shows little or no movement. Because of the inhibited muscular response (postural atonia), the body is totally relaxed and almost catatonic. Paradoxically, there is a heightened state of awareness and mental activity evidenced by brain waves, blood pressure, and pulse rate. EEG waves called PGO waves radiate from the **p**ons in the brain stem, through the **g**eniculate (visual) body into the **o**ccipital lobe (visual/associational area) of the cortex. These waves mean the dream theater is open for business!

At this point, our internal experience is as real as normal daily life, with only **two possible fundamental differences**. First, when we dream, our brain activates the muscular inhibition reflex (postural atonia), so we do not physically act out our dreams. We can dream of flying, walking, or running, and we do not actually get up and do those things. (If you are wondering if sleepwalking and other similar phenomena are a result of the brain stem failing to throw the muscular inhibition switch, you are right! In most cases, though, sleepwalking is not a result of people acting out their bizarre, REM dreams because it occurs during **non**-REM sleep.) Interestingly, as we mentioned earlier, the only muscles that are free to move while we are dreaming are those which move our eyes. This leads us to the second possible difference: that involved with **vision and other sensory information**. In dreams, almost all information is internally generated. For example, when we dream, our eyes are closed. We are not receiving visual input from "out there" as we do when we are awake. So, instead of external light waves stimulating receptors in our retinas, our brain is sending its own internal signals in the form of PGO waves.

In many respects, our external reality is only as real (or unreal) as what we see in our dreams. In both cases, we are essentially doing the same thing: we are constructing realities. So even in our waking reality what we see "out there" is a delusion. How could this be possible? Our eyes receive light waves which bounce off the object(s) in our line of vision. Our brain computes the light waves and checks this new information *against data already stored in our neurons.* The resulting match or mismatch determines whether we identify the object or not. Our identification depends less on the external information and more on the information we have stored internally.

Let's take it a step further and look at hypnosis to see how these distinctions become even fuzzier. Superficially, most of the stimulation in hypnosis (as in dreams) is internally generated. Of course, suggestions are made by the hypnotherapist, but quite often the subject simply incorporates this outside stimulation (the suggestions) into her own internal reality in a meaningful way. Subjects can do this with little, if any, interruption of the trance. This explains why vague, ambiguous language is often more effective for inducing trance than specific language. Why? Because we naturally "fill in" the ambiguity with our own stored images, sounds, thoughts, and feelings. Daydreams work the same way. Our focus is inward and we limit outside sensory information in favor of internally-generated representations.

Our experience with clients diagnosed with depression explains how this same process can go awry. One of the things we have notice with depressed people is that they spend far more time inside than outside. They are paying attention to an internally constructed reality, which becomes more and more detached from external, sensory experience. The information on which they are basing their feelings quickly becomes dated, because it is coming from impressions and memories that they have had in storage! Depression, as many other psychological problems, is a trance. Psychosis is a trance which does not flex very well from context to context. One of the obvious ways to interrupt depression, and other psychological disorders, is to bring the person outside and help them become involved in their current sensory experience. This will break the trance and wake them up from their bad dream!

In summary, the phenomenon of REM sleep, or dreaming, has important similarities to our waking reality and states. Certainly many of the physiological mechanisms of dreaming are quite similar to what happens in trance during the waking state. EEG (brain wave) activity in hypnosis correlates to alpha and theta activity. Hypnosis is also characterized by increased parasympathetic activity (relaxation). In this state our anterior hypothalamus inhibits the reticular activating system and facilitates the release of cholinergic cells which slow our internal processes. This decreases our awareness of our surroundings. What does all of this mean? It means that we begin to emphasize what is "inside" rather than what is "outside." Daydreams, trance, beliefs, even much of our objective sensory awareness is "filled in" with our "own stuff" from "inside." What is important is to ***develop the flexibility*** to blend the right mix of what is "outside" and what is internally generated to ***create new realities*** that further ***learning, growth, and evolution.***

Neuropeptides: Their Ebb And Flow In Dreaming

As we experience the peaks and valleys of our lives—the tenderness of a lover's touch, the majesty of a green wheat field being swept by the wind, the irritation of being cut off on the expressway, the exhilaration of riding white-water rapids, the grief of losing a loved one, or the comfort of curling up with a good book on a cold winter's evening—an intricate reality runs parallel to each of these experiences.

This intricate reality is the **chemistry of information**. One of the basic units in this system is a neuropeptide (we will later divide this information into smaller units). Every thought is accompanied by a neuropeptide. Neuropeptides are the "chemical messengers" which our physical body uses for internal communication. They are one of science's answers to the mind-body split because they bridge thoughts and physical reality. The same neuropeptides which exist in the brain also exist throughout the entire body. They are found in organs, tissues, and blood. Today, in scientific circles, the term "*neuro*peptide" is basically a misnomer. The term was coined when scientists thought peptides were located only in the brain and nervous system. However, more recently, scientists have documented that neuropeptides in fact move throughout the entire body.

This discovery gives credence to the notion that our thoughts are communicated automatically throughout our entire body via neurotransmitters. Every part of the body is communicating with every other part by means of these chemical messengers. If we are happy, our immune system is happy. If we are depressed, the functioning of our immune system may be depressed. Some investigators even say that these neuropeptides are not just the bridge between thought and the physical body: they **are** the physical manifestation of thought. They are one and the same. Whether our thoughts are separate but connected to our neuropeptides, or our thoughts and neuropeptides are different descriptions of the same thing, the fact is that when one changes the other also changes.

What relevance does this have to dreaming and the practices in this book? The answer is: more than you can think (that is safe when you really think about it!). Just as one specific neuropeptide may be correlated with one specific thought, so states of consciousness may be correlated with biochemical environments that are composed of many combinations and blends of various neuropeptides and neurotransmitters. The biochemical environment of sleep is different from the waking state. Likewise, the biochemistry of dreaming is different from other stages of sleep, and yet it is quite similar to the biochemistry of hypnosis.

Controlling The Tides Of Consciousness

There is truly an ebb and flow to the tides of chemical messages which wake us up, put us to sleep, help us dream, heal our bodies, and assist us in integrating new learnings. This ebb and flow of waking, sleeping, and dreaming is mediated by a certain class of neuropeptides, called "neuromodulators" which cause sweeping changes in the chemical environment of our brain. Neuromodulators set the tone for the actions of all the other neuropeptides. They set the tide which governs the behavior of all the lesser neuropeptides.

This model is known as the **Reciprocal Interaction Model**. At one end of the spectrum, aminergic cells, such as norepinephrine and serotonin, are in control when we are awake and alert. They modulate, or control, sympathetic arousal, which is the fight-and-flight response. At the other end of the spectrum, cholinergic cells, such as acetylcholine, are in control when we are dreaming. Acetylcholine modulates parasympathetic arousal, or the relaxation response. Acetylcholine allows for the loose associations which we make in our dreams. The part of the brain which is the source of these tides of consciousness is the *pons* located in the brain stem.

When we are awake, the amines keep acetylcholine in check. This makes it possible to track and record sensory input, and to stay oriented. The amines keep us from getting too "far out." During REM, the amines no longer restrain acetylcholine and "hallucinations" occur. The cholines create bizarre images, connections, and twists of reality which build dreams. Interestingly, people known as psychotics, who hallucinate during the waking state, have been found to have low levels of norepinephrine and serotonin and presumably higher levels of acetylcholine. So the amines contribute a great deal to the borders around our thinking which maintain our sanity. If these borders are too stringent we may become too linear and limited in the way we perceive the world.

Dream practices create pathways which enable us to vary our biochemistry at will and therefore change our realities. We have been asked, "Does that not happen any time a person changes her mind? Does a person not change her biochemistry since every thought corresponds with a particular neurotransmitter?" The answer is yes. But remember, all neuropeptides are not equal. It is one thing to make a ripple in an ocean. It is another thing to change the entire ocean and its ebb and flow. Dreaming practices have the potential to change the entire ocean! Changing the way we respond in our waking and dreaming realities will influence many "smaller" realities within them—i.e., our neurotransmitters.

For example, consider lucid dreaming. Lucid dreaming is the ability to be consciously aware of being in a dream while dreaming. It requires precision to wake up and know a dream is occurring, but at the same time remain in physiological sleep. At the point of lucidity, conscious choice abounds—as much as, if not more than, in the waking state, except that it occurs within the dream landscape. This is an awesome notion when we fully consider it. It is virtually unlimited! Why? **Because when we dream lucidly, we are voluntarily emitting norepinephrine with the assistance of our prefrontal lobe (our intention) while the tides are running in the opposite direction**. In the process, our pons receives the message and responds by sending up more norepinephrine. We have learned to precisely control the chemical tides in our mind with our intention. If we could teach this to people who have been diagnosed as psychotic, it is possible that they would no longer be psychotic, because they would be able to regain control over their attention to stop their hallucinations and delusions. Lucid dreamers use this same mechanism of controlling attention by becoming conscious of their dreams. Dream researchers hypothesize that understanding the mechanism for lucid dreaming and being able to use it, are the keys to unlocking psychosis! For the vast majority, lucidity and the other practices in this book are keys to unlocking realities which limit us, like "I cannot..." or "I will never..." Dream on...!

Let's take another example which, though less grand than unlocking psychosis, is fundamental to the basis of living a functional existence: learning. What is the relationship of learning to dreaming and the waking state? In simplistic terms, to learn something we first need to record or encode it. Secondly, we consolidate it so it becomes integrated with what we already know (so it becomes automatic), and afterwards we recall or use the information when it is needed. **To record information we need the amine tides**. But to **consolidate our learning, we need the cholinergic tides**, the dream tides. You may know someone, very close to you, who tried to cram the night before the big exam. Lots of coffee, little sleep. And maybe they got a decent grade, maybe not, but where did the information go after a day or two? It vanished. Why? There was not enough time for consolidation. That person you know, who is very close to you, might have benefitted in the long term with less coffee, and more sleeping and dreaming.

This misconception taken to the extreme is "sleep learning," where tapes are played during sleep to learn a new language (or new information). Many people who try this notice that not only do they not learn much, but they become confused about what they already knew *prior* to listening to the tapes. That is because sleep and dreaming, in particular, are great times for consolidation, but not for recording. The wrong tide for recording is running during sleep.

In REM our memory consolidates the new information it recorded earlier in the amine state. Researchers suspect that acetylcholine facilitates the conversion of short-term memory to long-term memory. It is as if the choline tide sweeps the information across all of the cortical circuits. It facilitates memory distribution across all kinds of circuits—even ones that do not make any sense, logically, but may be connected experientially—thereby creating the hyperassociations that characterize our dreams. Something else important happens during dreaming. Our brain—i.e. our unconscious mind—runs programs which automatically take the information we have recorded and integrate it with all the other information we had already stored. Widespread connections are made and rehearsed at the rate of six procedures (neural programs or neural motor programs) a second—and all of the rehearsals occur without the usual physical consequences! That is more than just learning. That is entertainment! Safe entertainment at that! Every reality we have, every dream we have, is inseparably "tide" to our chemistry. The reality is, however, that we sometimes forget who is regulating tides. That is the dream to break through.

Why Do We Dream? Science Gives It Its Best Shot

The bottom line (at the time of this book's publication) is that no one knows for sure why we dream! There are numerous models and belief systems which seek to explain why we dream but there is no definitive answer. One of the more progressive points of view comes from the brilliant work of two neuroscientists, J. Allan Hobson and Robert McCarley, who call their understanding the **Activation-Synthesis Hypothesis of Dreaming** (*American Journal Of Psychiatry 134,* 1977). We present this because we consider it the best explanation hard science, with its reductionistic tendencies, has to offer. It also points toward the limits of neuroscience and why we need to go further. This model is the psychological counterpart of the Reciprocal Interaction Model (the biochemistry model of the amine and choline tides above) that was the basis of our previous discussion.

According to Hobson and McCarley, dreaming activates the brain circuits—the foundation of consciousness. These "brain circuits beneath consciousness" are the neurological firings which originate from the pons in the brainstem and radiate throughout the cerebral cortices. These neurological firings are then interpreted by our higher cortical functions as dreams. Essentially our brain is **trying** to make sense or meaning from nonsense, i.e. "random" neurological pulsations emanating from our pons. While this is Hobson's position, and even though he is neutral about whether dreams themselves are really important or not, he has a habit of always recording his dreams—and he is not sure why he does it. Any ideas?

Hobson's point is interesting because it is similar to an exercise which we often use when we teach metaphor. In the "bushy brain" exercise in *Training Trances*, we ask two people to each simultaneously choose a word at random and say it aloud. The third person in the group then develops a response based upon what the two words have in common. This is the basis of how metaphor works: our mind interprets seemingly random events, and using our own life experiences, makes them meaningful. Even if Hobson and McCarley are correct, we still believe it is important to understand how and why our mind interprets these random impulses to make meaning, and what that meaning is. We will take this up in the interpretation section of this dream. What is important now is, ironically, the whole idea of random firings, which begs the question of "what" or "who" is producing the random firing?

To shed some light on this question, let's look at the findings of one of Hobson's predecessors, Wilder Penfield, and his famous studies on memory (*The Mystery Of The Mind*, 1975). Penfield is the often-cited neurosurgeon who performed surgical studies with epileptics by severing their corpus callosum to short-circuit the epilepsy. It was effective, but primitive by today's standards.

During the procedure, only the patient's skull was anesthetized, since the brain itself has no pain receptors. Penfield found that, when he electrically stimulated a specific point on the cerebral cortex, the patient began to relive a memory. He was looking for the engram (the memory trace) that would prove that memory was stored in a specific location in the brain. As he touched different areas, the patient vividly experienced different memories. After repeating this procedure with numerous patients he formed a number of conclusions, three of which are significant here. One was incorrect according to current research. One was plausible but virtually unprovable. And one was beyond anything science could handle!

Penfield's first conclusion was that memory has a specific location, and this was, as we have said, unsupported by current research. The brain seems to be organized along functional lines, as memories appear to be a product of networks of bioelectrical waves that resonate throughout the body-mind. Information is distributed simultaneously and redundantly throughout the entire body through neuropeptides, making a single location impossible.

His second conclusion was that everything we have ever experienced is recorded in our brain. Not only is this possible, it is a useful belief to have, but hard to validate. And in most cases it is easier to disprove than to prove scientifically.

Penfield's third conclusion is the least known and perhaps the most significant—it certainly is to this dream. It was that **we are more than simply the sum of our memories, our brain and body, our tissues and our chemistry**. During his experiments, Penfield would ask the patients about their memories and they would describe them in full sensory detail. They were, by all accounts, living the memory. Yet they also had a simultaneous awareness of being in the operating room. Here is the twister! He would ask them if they could fully experience the memory and simultaneously be in the operating room, and they could do both. When he asked them who was doing both things at once, the person in the operating room or the one in memory, they said it was a third person—whom some call "the choice maker," a witness or observer who is beyond the material body; a "consciousness" that is present and operates through pure intention. In other words, "someone else" was playing the instrument. So, to answer our question about the dreaming—"Who is doing the random firing?"—we need to move beyond Newtonian "hard science," and look to ancient wisdom and the "modern mysticism" of quantum physics, which also has something to say about why we dream at all.

Conscious Review Of Chapter 2

1. **We all have four or five dream periods per night.**

2. **The same cycle that causes us to dream at night functions throughout the day**. It repeats itself about sixteen times a day. Each period lasts from ninety to one hundred minutes. It is called the Ultradian Rhythm or the Basic Rest and Activity Cycle (BRAC).

3. **Trance and dreaming or rapid eye movement (REM), and the hypnogogic and hypnopompic states, are all similar**. All are marked by a generalized shift to parasympathetic arousal (i.e. the relaxation response) and subdominant hemispheric functioning.

4. **During the hypnopompic state we can recall our dreams**. Keep as still as possible when you first awaken to remain in this state and so remember your dreams.

5. **The closer we get to the morning, the more we dream**. These are the dreams you will remember most easily. Practice lucid dreaming at this time. Since you are then spending more time dreaming, it will be more likely that you realize you are in a dream.

6. **Every thought we have is communicated to every part of our physical body**. Each thought has a neuropeptide which accompanies it. Neuropeptides are the "chemical messengers" our physical body uses for internal communication.

7. **We can learn to control the ebb and flow of waking, sleeping, and dreaming.** The ebb and flow is mediated by neuromodulators which cause sweeping changes in the chemical environment of our brain. Aminergic cells, such as norepinephrine and serotonin, are in control when we are awake and alert. They modulate or control sympathetic arousal, which is the fight-and-flight response. Cholinergic cells, such as acetylcholine, take charge when we are dreaming.

8. **When we dream lucidly we are controlling the "tides" of our brain.** Lucid dreaming is voluntarily emitting norepinephrine with the assistance of our prefrontal lobe (our intention) while the tides are running in the opposite direction.

9. **Use sleep and dreams to consolidate learning** (cholinergic tides).

10. **Use the waking state to record information** (amine tides).

11. **We are more than just the sum of our memories, our brain and body, our tissues, and our chemistry** (the Penfield research).

Unconscious Review Of Chapter 2

As you are consciously looking at this page, it is your unconscious mind that is reading. You do not have to...***be aware***...of the complex chemical changes occurring at the unconscious level. Why should you? Your conscious mind can...sit back...and relax...for a moment and while your unconscious...mind can generate meaningful associations for your enjoyment and learning...that you experience cycles within cycles...each day you ride the tide of activity...while the rest...happens automatically ...all the while, more and more meaningful...associations...can be made without your awareness to increase your inner ***alignment***.

Now...we really do not know whether...you will remember...to use that state just before you fall asleep tonight to suggest that...you will ***remember*** your dreams in the morning. We do know that going into a trance now...or later...going into a meditation...now or later...going into a ***dream*** now or ***later***...can all accomplish the same thing. And what you can remember is that dreams can have lasting, profound, and beneficial effects that can stay with you for the rest...of your life.

And while you are sleeping deeply you do not have to... remember...***healing*** is taking place in every cell of your body. You can just sleep and the healing will ***happen***...as automatically as you can...dream...vivid dreams...as automatically and as predictably as the tides...that control the sea of dreams and all that is in them. The constant ebb and flow...give and take...the gentle push and pull of...***intention...***and...***acceptance***...all of which spring from a source...***deep within you***...and yet, beyond ***you***...that brings life...to ideas...thoughts...feelings and actions...that at first you may not understand or...fully appreciate...just yet that they...have a life...of their own...just as a rose bud blooms...there is nothing you need to do but...pay attention...and...watch it ***bloom...naturally,*** as its beauty becomes real and meaningful...simply because you have observed it into being.

Chapter 3

Quantumfying Dreaming:
Consciousness And The Other Stuff Of Dreaming

This chapter discusses what quantum physics has to do with dreams and reality. First, let us tell you that we are not experts in quantum physics, and do not purport to be. In fact, our understanding is that a true quantum physicist, who claims to understand it all, would either have to be lying or deeply troubled! Paraphrasing Niels Bohr, one of the founding fathers of quantum physics, **"Anyone who is not truly disturbed by the conclusions of quantum physics does not truly understand it"** (Wheatley, 1994).

We include this brief section because of its heuristic value. It makes us think! It makes us step outside the dream of reality that most of us experience—the reality colored by Isaac Newton, religion, and our own personal histories. For us, it reflects the paradoxical, seemingly nonsensical, contradictory, holographic, mysterious, orderly, and perfect (hopefully!) nature of what **IS**. We should mention that the quantum physics description of reality is no more valid that any other model. It is still just a description, just a metaphor among many others. However, what is different about quantum physics is that its description transcends itself. That is worth contemplating. Because of this, quantum physics now serves as a bridge from the physical and psychological to the spiritual realities that inspired us to write this dream.

The field of quantum physics grew from a question that was a logical extension of Newtonian physics. The latter was a mechanistic, reductionistic way of looking at how the physical world operated. By reducing the unknown to the predictable, the known, with the expectation that all things could be reduced in the same way, Newton transformed humankind, so much so that by the turn of the twentieth century, physics was rapidly becoming a closed science. Scientists thought they had all the answers to explain how things worked. There were only a few concepts that needed elaboration and that would take care of everything. The first, which is of interest to this dream, was the question that gave birth to quantum physics. It involved the nature of light: specifically, how does light interact with the electrons in a metal? Have you ever wondered why black objects glow red when heated, and why, at certain temperatures, the red glow becomes blue? We are not sure if we have ever given these ideas much conscious thought, but many scientists at the turn of the century were consumed by the "black body puzzle."

When physicists searched for the missing piece of this puzzle, it seemed to be lying...where else but inside Pandora's box! At the time, scientists on every continent were studying the nature of light, and not only as it related to the "black body puzzle." A number of physicists, when studying light in its most elementary form (photons), discovered simultaneously that at times light behaves as a **particle** and at other times it behaves as a **wave**. Likewise, an electron at times behaves as an object and at other times it behaves as a non-object because it has no dimension! Therefore the term "quantum" was coined to describe a wave-particle or energy packet, a "wavicle."

These scientists noticed that **whether the electron "is" a wave or a particle depends upon the context in which it is observed and how it is observed**. As you might guess, this catapulted the secure, logical, mechanical, and objectified world described by Newton into a moving maze of mirrors where the observer could not be removed yet still see a reflection. Quantum physics had dissolved the difference between "field" and "matter" or, for our purposes, thought and matter. The "field" is unlimited potentiality. It is pure information. It has no form as we know it. It exists only in the form of probabilities. What turns this field into matter is measurement. In fact, the words "matter" and "measurement" come from the same Greek word *metra* which means "uterus." **Thought gives birth to matter through measurement**. Our thoughts behave as wave forms until we identify with them. Prior to our thoughts, all that exists is pure potential. It is everything that is, because it is nothing. It is unexpressed potential ceaselessly interacting with itself.

When we have a thought, we are picking up on one possibility, or frequency, within the entire field or universe, called the "frequency domain." It is similar to a radio antenna which can theoretically pick up all of the possible radio waves which exist. These possibilities exist in the form of frequencies, or radio waves. Only when we actually turn on the radio and adjust the tuner can we actualize these possibilities, whether it is music, news, or sports in which we are interested. Turning on the radio and adjusting the tuner transforms the radio waves from possibility to reality. Our thoughts work the same way.

A thought is a disturbance in the field. It is a tiny pebble cast into a still pond. It is a form in the formless. It yields an effect both inside and outside us. The effect created will depend upon how much energy the thought has and how much we energize it with our "ego" or personality. This is when the conversion occurs—what was pure potential takes form as a thought when we **identify** with it. Identification creates material reality. We have thoughts that range from joyous to unhealthy to vengeful to enlightened. They are all examples of what we may pull from the frequency domain. All of these thoughts are expressions of pure potential.

When we identify with our thoughts they behave like particles—they are born into the world of matter or neuropeptides. One way in which we identify with these thoughts is by making judgements about ourselves by thinking, "Oh, because this thought occurred, it must mean that I am..." (you fill in the blank). At the moment of identification, the thought is transformed from a wave into matter, perhaps in the form of a feeling. The more we focus on the feeling, the more "real" it becomes. It interacts with "itself" and produces motivation or action, which then leads to increased physicality, or grounding of the original wave form. The thought becomes a deed. Look around. Everything that we are experiencing began with a thought. Since we can experience it, it means that sufficient energy was present to bring it into the material world.

How Does This Relate To Dreams And Dreaming?

Both our dreaming reality and our waking reality come from the same place. They are two major examples of how reality is created from the formless. They both follow the same blueprint of creation and evolution that we described earlier. However, our dreams at night are often bizarre, crazy, and illogical compared to our waking reality. When we sleep, our minds shift and meander through a virtually unlimited landscape of associations where there are no guardrails on reality, no yellow or white lines to direct traffic! During our waking realities, the guardrails are back in place. We have time, space, and matter to keep us buckled safely in our seats. We have religion, science, cultural "norms," laws, and most of all, consensual reality, to keep things logical, secure, and predictable.

While both realities come from the same source, our point of view is that our night dreams are closer to the source itself. Ultimately, they are probably more similar than they are different, at least according to the quantum physics model. It is just that the form of our night dreams makes it easier for us to see beyond everyday waking reality and its constraints. Our dreaming reality backs us into the source, where fewer constructs, constraints, and limitations exist.

In our dreams we can be talking to our boss in the house in which we lived as a child, turn around, and be standing by a mountain lake. We can be a full-grown adult and find ourselves naked in a high-school class. We can have illuminating conversations with people whom we have never met in our waking reality. We can talk to dead people who are alive and well in our dreams, and we do not bat an eyelash. Anything can be connected to anything. Our dreams echo the conclusions quantum physicist, David Peat, had on reality as a whole, "No physical process connects two physical states of being, no duration of time separates them" (*Einstein's Moon*, 1990). In our nightdreams we experience this profound truth. It is not just a questionable proposition that we can consider, analyze, and dismiss. In our dreams, we live this reality. It becomes part of our experience, although we may not value it in our waking reality. This is not to say that we should rush out and live our waking lives with the same abandon and chaotic energy that we live our dream lives. But it is a pointer. It points to other possibilities—possibilities that we may not be able to materialize immediately, but which perhaps form the horizon where one reality meets the other.

When we visit Hawaii, we carry out a sunset ritual. We stand on the smooth, black lava flows which jut out into the Pacific, and we watch the sun make its slow descent into the water and beyond. As we look at the sun, we outstretch our arms, cupping our hands and cradling the sun's image. We breathe in the sun's energy as we pull our hands toward us. Exhaling, we let go of whatever we want to release from our lives. The horizon is the limit of our vision—where the red sun leaves the blue sky and merges with the ocean. There is a moment at the end when only the last yellowish-red glimmer balances on the shimmering water. Hawaiians say it is a doorway—the last opening before the door closes. "Send all of your offerings at that moment," they say, "and the I'o, the one God, will transform them as they go back to their Source. They will no longer be yours." In those moments we connect with the sun. The rays that touch our eyes connect us to it.

All of us have had moments like this. Flashes occur where we feel the interconnectedness. Are we really interconnected? We think so. Many physicists do, too. But if we are all interconnected, why is it not more evident in practical ways, in our everyday lives? It can be quite confusing. On one level we are separate and on another we are interconnected. How could this be? Where *is* the horizon where religion and science meet? Just follow the waving particle: it is back to the quantum again.

Reality Is Observer Created

In the 1920s, Werner Heisenberg, Irwin Schroedinger and Niels Bohr, the founding fathers of quantum physics, suggested that subatomic particles come into existence **only** in the presence of an observer. Another important and perplexing finding which surfaced at that time was that when certain subatomic processes occur they create a pair of particles with identical properties. No matter how far apart these particles move, they have identical angles of polarization. It is as if these two particles can communicate their coordinates to each other instantly while changing directions. Their movements always covary exactly. This created an interesting challenge, because, if they can communicate instantly, then that communication has to be faster than light. However, this violated a fundamental principle embraced by physicists, including Albert Einstein, which claimed that nothing could exceed the speed of light. Here we go again! Another paradox in science. First it was the waving particle and now it is things moving faster than the speed of light. How were scientists going to get themselves out of this one?

Einstein and his colleagues, Podolsky and Rosen, took the direct approach. They set out to prove that Bohr was wrong—after all, they suggested, nothing could exceed the speed of light. However, Bohr's point was never that the communication, or information, between the particles (as separate entries) was moving faster than light. His main argument was that Einstein had forgotten that until subatomic particles are observed, they do not exist. Bohr said Einstein was wrong because the latter was thinking about these twin "particles" as *separate* entities. So the issue was not really speed or movement because the particles were not separate in the first place. They had not been observed yet—they were still an undifferentiated part of an interconnected whole. Until they were observed, they would be the formless backdrop from which everything in reality emerged. Only observation and subsequent conceptualization made them separate.

As it turned out, most of the physics community agreed with Bohr, but more for technical reasons pertaining to errors in Einstein's experimental design. (We will spare you the details!) **The critical point is that we observe things into being**. Otherwise, what is unobserved remains an undifferentiated and uninterrupted interconnected whole.

Reality Is Holographic

Physicist David Bohm (yet another physicist!) framed this finding in a simplified way while expanding its significance to explain many mysteries of the universe (*Wholeness And The Implicate Order*, 1980). One theorist commented that while Bohm's theory is just a theory, it is so intuitively satisfying that he hopes it turns out to be true. **Bohm's explanation is based upon the notion that the universe is a giant hologram**.

Just like a holographic image, each piece of the universe has within it the same pattern as the whole. Bohm proposed that there are two orders of reality: the explicate order and the implicate order. **The explicate order is our level of existence**. It is created through our observation and measurement. In the explicate we can conceptualize two photons moving exactly in relation to each other. It is a level of duality because by means of our observation we have brought something into existence. In order for something to exist, it must also have its non-mirror-image reverse, its multi-dimensional opposite. For example, for "security" to exist, by presupposition "not security" must also exist. Put more simply, if we are constantly striving for "success," we are in some way acknowledging the existence of "not success."

The second and deeper level of reality that Bohm referred to is the "implicate order." **The implicate is the unobserved level of reality**. It is pure potential. At this level all is still possible as it has not yet been expressed in the explicate. The implicate is referred to as the "Void" in Buddhism; the "Akasha" in Hinduism; and the "I'o" in Hawaiian spirituality. All possibilities are enfolded in this quantum reality. This is the source of all creation and the destination of everything that transforms from the physical (death). It is the level on which everything is interconnected. Separateness occurs only at the level of the explicate.

Here is a way to think about this: imagine you have in front of you two separate TV monitors—the totality of your reality. In each monitor you see a fish with similar colors, but different shapes. Whenever you see one fish move, you see the other fish move in precise relation to it. It is as if the fish are communicating instantaneously through the space between the monitors, so that they always know where and how the other is moving. This is the explicate level of reality. This interpretation of reality assumes that because we see two fish in two separate monitors, they must be separate.

What if you later discovered that you were observing the **same** fish captured by two cameras from two different angles? The two fish that appeared earlier to be moving in relation to each other were just one fish! Their communication was not breaking the light barrier. At this "deeper" level the two fish are one and the same. This deeper level is the implicate level of reality.

Therefore, Bohm believed an electron was not one thing but a totality or ensemble enfolded through the whole of space. An electron appears to be moving due to a continuous series of enfoldments and unfoldments. There is a constant interchange between the implicate and explicate orders. The way an observer interacts with the ensemble determines which aspect of the electron unfolds and which remains hidden.

Many of us go through our lives forgetting that sensation and perception create separateness. We have been conditioned to believe in separateness and therefore disconnect ourselves from the unlimited information and potentiality of which the universe is made. By the way, do not get us wrong here—we are not saying that we should deny the reality that humanity has built and think that we can walk through walls just because we know the quantum truth. As we are fond of saying, even quantum physicists live their everyday lives according to Newtonian physics. It is one thing to "know" this intellectually and it is quite another to live it and experience it in the eternal now! But, we **are** all much more than we "think" we are. We often unknowingly divide the universe and create things (concepts, beliefs, and realities) and, in doing so, often make it seem as though "they" have a life of their own. In the process we can become "victims" of our own creations and constructions.

"As above, so below" is taught in many shamanic and spiritual disciplines. The macrocosm reflects the microcosm and vice versa. This idea of interconnectedness is not reserved for all of the New Agers and students of metaphysics. This idea is now considered fact, because it no longer needs to rely on quantum theory to prove its veracity. Could it be that all of the bizarre episodes and possibilities that occur in dreams are actually clearer glimpses of how reality really works on the quantum level? Bell's Theorem, developed by the physicist John Stuart Bell, is a landmark discovery because it proves mathematically that there are no local causes in the universe (Bell, 1964). The literal translation is that cause-effect does not exist. If cause-effect does not exist, then time does not exist either. Therefore our everyday concepts of reality no longer suffice.

And there is more! Consider one of the conclusions reached by another famed physicist, Richard Feynman (Herbert, 1985). He proved mathematically that everything that might have happened influences everything that does happen. To determine the probability of an event, he took all the possible probabilities that could occur, and discovered that certain probabilities will cancel one another out because they are opposites. What is left is a wave whose points indicate what will actually happen.

Therefore, from a quantum physics point of view we can say that the future, not the past, actually determines the present. What if there is an important person whom we will be meeting at an unspecified time in the future? For this meeting to occur, certain events in the present need to take place so that our paths actually cross. For the future to occur, the present has to align itself to make this happen. If this seems beyond the realm of possibility then take comfort in the spirit of Bohr's comment which we referred to earlier: "If you are not totally shocked and abhorred by what you learn in quantum physics, then you truly do not understand it" (Wheatley, 1994).

To expand our thinking even further, the notion of past, present, and future is a moot point. At the level of the quantum there is no time. Time only appears when we try to measure change in the explicate. Whether you realize it or not, you have never been anywhere other than now. **When have you not been in now**? Now is all there is. Our consciousness may not be operating on this level, but now is all there is. Living in the past or the future is only a simulation we can masterfully create and hypnotize ourselves into believing.

We Dream To Create

Fred Alan Wolf, a physicist and author of *The Dreaming Universe* (1994), postulates that the universe dreamed itself into existence. He is in good company here! Many ancient cultures have espoused this view. In the Yogavasistha, a sacred Hindu text, dreaming sleep is described as the opportunity for human beings to create as the gods create, by emitting images. Just as the Divine forces dreamed the universe into existence, humans constantly "dream" their own worlds into existence. Just as the images created by the Divine enfold (recede into) a more profound reality, so do those created by the human dreamer. Holographically, our dreams are the microcosm for how the universe, the macrocosm, created itself.

In our dreaming reality all that exists is thought, just thought expressing itself. If we wake up in the morning experiencing a certain emotion, it is because our thought patterns during sleep had sufficient energy to ground the feeling into physical reality. This is no longer only the realm of thought, because the physical sensation has crossed over into our waking consciousness. If, upon arising, we start doing things because of this emotion, then it grounds itself even more deeply into our waking reality. In many cases it is not really important whether we remember the source of the emotion in the dream. We may be completely amnesic with regard to the dream content, yet it still exerts an influence on us. It sets the tone for the day. On the negative side, this is "getting up on the wrong side of the bed." Maybe other times we wake up and feel tremendous. These feelings have an effect on our conscious waking thoughts and affect how we go about our day. Every night when we dream, we experience the process of creation whether we realize it or not.

Did you know that infants dream far more than adults do? It is true. In fact fetuses are in REM sleep for about fifteen hours a day. After birth they spend eight hours a day dreaming. Why? What are they doing dreaming all the time? They are dreaming to create. On the physical level they are dreaming to grow a healthy brain. On a psychological level they are rehearsing. What are they rehearsing? They are rehearsing who they will be when they wake up. They are, in effect, dreaming themselves into existence. They are creating and rehearsing the personality with which they come to identify. The neural connections and the meaning created and rehearsed during REM are expressed through their thoughts and actions. These actions then become self-referential; they refer to the possibilities created in the dream state and become the stuff of future dreams. As this cycle of creation, rehearsal, and expression rolls on, they create the concept of the self and of life.

So each night as we dream we are creating multiple realities. Some we never remember; others we do remember. All of these have an effect on our waking reality. What we will discuss next is how we can use our connection with the quantum field and dreaming to transform our waking reality. How do we take these lofty concepts and ground them into our everyday reality? Like most of the important things in life, it is simpler than you might think.

Conscious Review Of Chapter 3

1. **We observe things into being**. Whether the electron "is" a wave or a particle depends upon the context in which it is observed and how it is observed.

2. **Thought gives birth to matter through measurement**. Our thoughts behave as wave forms until we identify with them. Prior to our thoughts all that exists is pure potentiality. The words "matter" and "measurement" come from the same Greek root *metra* which means "uterus."

3. **When we identify with our thoughts they behave like particles.** They are born into the world of matter or neuropeptides. The more thought and energy we put into something the more material it becomes.

4. **Both our dreaming reality and our waking reality come from the same place**. They both are creations whose source is the quantum field or the Void. In many ways dreaming is a closer representation of reality at the deepest level. Dreams, like the Void, transcend time, space, energy, and matter.

5. **Reality is holographic**. **At the deepest level we are all one**. Like a holographic image, each piece of the universe has within it the same pattern as the whole. There are two orders of reality: the explicate and the implicate. The explicate is our level of existence. It is created through our observation and measurement. The second and deeper level of reality is the "implicate order." The implicate is the unobserved level of reality. It is pure potentiality. This is the source of all creation.

6. **We dream to create**. In the Yogavasistha, a sacred Hindu text, dreaming sleep is described as the opportunity for human beings to create as the gods create, by emitting images. Fetuses are in REM sleep for about fifteen hours a day. After birth they spend eight hours a day dreaming. We, as humans, are dreaming to create our selves.

7. **Each night we dream we are creating multiple realities**. We are creating what quantum physicists call "parallel universes." They are all occurring simultaneously along with our waking state including its past and future memories.

Unconscious Review Of Chapter 3

As you finish reading this chapter, we do not know how much it has caused you to ***stretch*** your thinking about ***reality***...your life or other things. We do know that after having read a satisfying amount of this book, you will eventually put it down. And when you do, no longer observing it, its contents and information will once again be enfolded deeply within its pages and its cover. Knowing that its information will be brought into being the next time you read it, and its contents are unfolded before you—this book itself has no meaning and therefore no reality beyond which you, the reader, give it. It is your experience, your observation that ***creates the meaning***.

In the same way, as you lie down to sleep and your conscious mind begins to unravel the thoughts of the day...you might even ***wonder***...which of those thoughts will recede back into the Void from which they came...never to be observed again, and which ones will become the basis for new creations in your life.

In the same way as you eventually fall asleep, your conscious mind recedes enfolded within the covers of sleep...sleep deeply...and prepares to ***create new realities*** that you call your dreams. ***Dreams of creation*** built only of thought...thought pulled from the middle of nowhere...knowhere you have been...***knowhere you are***...knowhere you are going...a dream...a reality...brought into creation merely by your thought...

Now, we do not know what kind of ***productive dreams*** you will have tonight, or how much you will ***remember your dreams***... Perhaps you might be surprised to find...that...you ***realize that you are in a dream*** while you are in one...and ***you ask, "Is this a dream?"***...Maybe you will create a book that you will be reading and you will not be able to read its words clearly and you ***ask yourself, "Is this a dream?"*** or maybe you will just go on creating new possibilities for creative solutions for your waking life. We do not know. We only know that you will dream tonight and each night you live a parallel life...

And have you ever thought about what it would be like to have a ***continuous awareness*** of that reality in the same way you do in your waking state?

Chapter 4

Incubation:

Growing Intention In The Quantum Field

Quantum physics aside, there is a lot one can learn from growing plants. *Often what can take the longest is deciding what plant you want to grow and for what purpose. The choices are virtually unlimited. You can look around and see what others have grown, pick from catalogs, or even go to garden centers that have large seed sections with an astronomical variety from which to choose. If you are growing the plant from seed, you need to know what it will look like when it is mature and ready to flower, bear fruit, and reproduce. The easiest thing to do is to get a picture of it. Of course, there is no resemblance between the seed and the picture of the fully grown plant on the seed packet. You have to trust that this small nondescript seed will actually grow into the picture you have. So you make your selection and choose something that you really like.*

Next you have to find the right time and place to do the planting. It needs to have the right conditions to grow: climate, season, and location. Growing corn in the middle of winter in the north-eastern United States is probably not advisable. You might be able to do it in a greenhouse, but it will take a lot of time and energy to make it work.

However, if you plant corn seeds in late spring in the north-east, you can achieve results with a lot less effort. Some people who live in even colder climates successfully grow tropical plants in their homes, but it takes a lot of skill. While trying to grow something exotic and unusual can be fun, we prefer growing plants that are indigenous to our area, suited to our soil and climate. That way we have more time to do other things.

When the time is right to plant the seed, make sure that it has the space it needs to grow. If you plant too many seeds too closely together, they may not all grow. One policy that many farmers follow, is to always plant more than you expect to get. Of course, very few farms grow only one thing. They grow different crops in different fields and keep them separate. They also believe in letting some fields lie fallow, so they can rest for a season. This replenishes the soil with nutrients to grow crops next season.

Once you plant a seed, you water it, give it the proper amount of light, and give it some time. This is where trust comes in again. Once it is under the soil you have to let go of it. If you keep digging it up to check its progress you will interrupt its natural tendency to grow and evolve. Even though you cannot see what is going on beneath the surface there is a lot going on. The seed will be nourished by the soil surrounding it.

Depending on your familiarity with the plant you want to grow, you may or may not know how soon it will pop up above the soil. Different seeds have different germination periods; some happen overnight, others take days, or even longer. Once it breaks the surface, then you can appreciate it and watch it grow. Keep watering it. From time to time you might have to prune if it is growing erratically. You might need to stake it for extra support. As you observe it, you will know what adjustments need to be made, based upon how well it is growing. One thing to remember, though, is, when you make an adjustment, you really need to give the plant a few days before you make another one. As the plant matures, you still need to give it attention, but probably less frequently, because by then it is strong enough to sustain itself for longer periods. It has what it needs to live and will continue growing on its own. Nature takes its course. You probably already know that most plants will grow in the direction of light. Sometimes in its insistence upon growing toward the light a plant may become unbalanced. It may need to be turned slightly, so that its structure stays solid and centered to facilitate further growth.

Eventually your plant will bear fruit. Many times more than just one piece of fruit. How do you know which one to pick? Most farmers do not decide ahead of time to pick the third piece on the lower left branch or the second one on the lowest branch. They wait until they see one that is ripe and they pick it. They also realize that if they pick all of the fruit they plant, they may have no other way to reproduce that fruit. They always leave some on the vine for future growing seasons and, if they have more than they need, they give it away for others to enjoy.

The Breakfast Of Masters

As we begin the next section of this dream, we want to tell you that there are some common elements which are relevant to all dreaming practices. The three primary elements which we cover in this book are: incubation, interpretation, and lucidity. All of these practices will be greatly enhanced by the information we have included in this section, **The Breakfast Of Masters.**

As we have studied dream systems and spiritual systems in general, we looked for the fundamental distinctions between truly "enlightened masters" and the rest of us on the path. While there are many other distinctions than those we have cited, these are the ones that are most important in the development of dreaming practices.

Intention

The first is intention. Enlightened masters have sharpened their **intention** so they are really **one-pointed**. This means **the ability to focus and maintain one's attention and purpose over time**. While this process begins as a deliberate conscious act, it is really more than that. One-pointedness refers to the ability of the conscious, unconscious, and higher conscious minds to act in total alignment, synergistically, and simultaneously.

Intention is like a laser beam which cuts through all the fluff. It begins with a clearly focused thought about an action we want to take or something we want to produce. If our intention is clear then we are actually first creating the results we want in our mind. We see the results in our mind's eye, and the results of the results, and we know that this is what we want. With certain masters, when the intention is absolutely clear, it is as if they send out a "telepathic cord" into the future which actually creates the event at that point. Often they only need to "intend" something and it just occurs. This is a result of their inner clarity and of many years of consistent practice in focusing their intention.

If our intention does not create spontaneous results then we need to follow through with action. Our intention is made concrete through our actions. If our intention is not strong enough then it is most likely that we will not follow through with action. In this case, we call this a "desire" rather than an intention. Strengthening our intention, through clarity and focus, over time produces remarkable results. Because of this we believe that our intention is the single most powerful thing we can use to produce the results we want in our lives. In the end intention is everything.

living in tension versus living intention

Generally when there is a discrepancy between conscious and unconscious intention, the unconscious intention will prevail. Sometimes though, we may go back and forth between conscious intention and unconscious intention. In this case conflict may arise between the conscious and unconscious minds and they will be "in tension." We frequently see this with people who want to exercise, lose weight, and get in shape. They set fitness goals for themselves but find it tough to follow through. Why? While their conscious mind thinks that it is a good idea to do these things, their unconscious mind may find them boring, depriving, and unfulfilling. At the unconscious level of intention there is nothing that is particularly compelling about these goals.

The relationship of conscious and unconscious intention can be cybernetic. What we intend consciously will affect what we intend unconsciously and vice versa. Exercise is a good example. Overall we may be motivated to exercise on a daily basis, but there may be times when we just do not feel like doing it even though we are well rested. We even know that we will enjoy it or feel better once we get started and we still do not feel like doing it. This is an instance where using our conscious intention can be instrumental. If we focus our conscious intention we can get over this temporary bump and get back on track. The point is that it is a temporary bump; it is short-term in nature. However, if we feel unmotivated most of the time when we think about exercising then something is wrong. In this case, we either need to check in with our unconscious mind to discover what its intention is in not being motivated to exercise, or we need to make our goal more realistic.

The ideal for intention is to be so one-pointed that we do not have to make distinctions between our conscious, unconscious, and higher conscious minds. If we collapse the distinctions, the relationship of the three minds is no longer cybernetic; it is simultaneous and one-pointed. Most of us have had times when our intention was one-pointed. We set our intention and it was fulfilled. Things just seemed to flow and did so in a way that we could have never explicitly planned. Each piece fell into place as it should, and that is living intention. It is worthwhile thinking back and identifying those times. Think about them before and after incubating a dream, and it will activate the associations to support the direction you set in your incubation.

Energy

The second quality common to enlightened masters is the amount of **energy** they have or are able to move through their bodies. **They have the ability to transmit a significant amount of energy to others**. This could be for the purposes of passing knowledge and information, effecting healing, or opening up the neurology of the recipient. This is not to say that all of us do not have the ability to transmit energy to others. We do. In fact, it would be hard to think of when we do not transmit energy to others! The difference, once again, is in degree. As most of us have discovered, any spiritual discipline takes energy. Dream practices are no exception. If we are tired from working all day or not getting enough sleep, we may not have the energy it takes to remember our dreams. If we are practicing lucidity, it takes a fair amount of energy to pierce through the barrier between our waking and dream states so we can be consciously aware in our dreams. There are numerous ways to build energy, including diet, exercise, postures, breathing techniques, meditation, and the use of symbols. Going into these in any detail is, however, beyond the scope of this book.

What we will say is that the **connection between intention and energy is central**. To a large degree our intention guides the flow of energy. Intention, starting with a thought, plus energy equals creation. The more we are able to handle greater and greater amounts of energy, the more likely it is that we will be able to turn thought into matter. However, energy without steady intention leads to chaos and creations that are not really congruent. Sharpening intention increases the likelihood that we can attract and steer the energy in the direction we want it to go.

- Don Juan and Carlos Castaneda

A useful illustration of the relationship of intention to energy comes from the work of Carlos Castaneda (1984, 1987, 1993: see Bibliography for details). Carlos's teacher, don Juan, often spoke of the principle of impeccability. In his system, impeccability is the economical use of energy. Wasting energy is an indulgence of the ego. **Impeccability means putting total intention into whatever is being done in order to complete the task with minimum amounts of energy**. According to don Juan and many other systems, unresolved negative emotions, conflicts, and incompletes from the past are the biggest energy drains. These lead to indulgences of the ego gone astray. The "warrior of knowledge" is freed through impeccability to use energy for dreaming practices and transcendence. In the waking state, he develops disciplined intention. This ensures that when the warrior is ready to enter other realities, he can approach new realities with the same impeccability.

- The Hawaiian System

Hawaiian Huna offers another principle that is similar, but more eloquent in its simplicity. A student once asked a Kahuna, "What do Kahunas eat?" expecting that the Kahuna would outline some esoteric diet plan. The Kahuna replied, "We eat whatever we feel like eating," and walked away. What did he mean? It all goes back to the original name for Huna (ancient Hawaiian psychology): Ho'omana. Roughly translated "Ho'o" means "to make" and "mana" means "energy." Hence Ho'omana means "to make energy." Additionally, "Huna" means "secret." So Hawaiian Huna was the "secret of how to make energy."

The guiding principle in this ancient system is the question, **"Will this raise or lower my energy?"** Are we thinking or doing things that will raise or lower our energy? We have found this to be extremely useful in many facets of our everyday lives. It cuts through the fluff. While it is not always easy to follow through with the answer to the question, it is a damned good one to ask. It is what the Kahuna was referring to in his reply. In some cases he might eat pork, in others, taro or fish. It would depend on the circumstances and his energy at the time. Many Kahunas, before making an important decision, would do two things: breathe to increase energy and ask, "Will the results of this decision raise or lower my energy?"

The Ego Meter

The third key that truly enlightened masters possess is affectionately referred to as the "ego meter." An enlightened master acknowledges that, **"I am more than I think I am"** and **"I am really not the one doing it anyway."** Otherwise, we limit our actions only to what we conceive ourselves to be—our ego. This is one of the differences between "white magic" and "black magic" as we conceptualize it. In black magic, the practitioners believe they are the sole source of the energy and power. They deny that they are instruments for a source much greater than themselves. In the case of healers who believe that they are the ones who actually do the healing, they run the risk of burning themselves out. As a good friend of ours once said, "If you use your personal energy to do healing, it is just a matter of time until you find a client who has more than you do."

In that case, what do you do? Recognize that you are not really the one who is doing the healing. This is what a "white magician" believes. We happen to be the instrument through which the energy flows. Our job is to cultivate our nervous system so that it is a clean, precise instrument that the energy can use to do its healing work. It is not up to us to heal someone. That is way beyond us. It is up to us only to do our best to create the best possible environment for healing to occur. In some cases that may simply mean getting out of the way!

Dreaming practices work the same way. Through our own experience we recognize that our ability to proceed has a lot to do with who we think we are, as well as our motives for doing the practices. It is always useful to remember, **"You are not doing it by yourself,"** and **"No matter what you think you are, you are always more than that."**

Dream Incubation

Dream incubation is the process of consciously intending the type or function of a dream you want to have, before you actually have it. Perhaps you are wondering why you would want to practice dream incubation? Would you like to be more creative? Would you like to increase your recall of dreams? Would you like to resolve personal issues, "doing therapy on the nightshift," as we mentioned earlier? Would you like to do all of this while you rest comfortably and sleep? What if we told you that it would require less than five to ten minutes of your time? Are you interested? If you are willing to invest more time, how about learning to create your own dreamscapes or scenarios where you meet guides, teachers, or others you have never met, but from whom you want to learn and model? Do you want to receive messages from your Higher Self? Develop lucidity? All of these are possibilities, depending on your level of interest and commitment. In the dream system outlined in this book, as many of the others we have studied, incubation is the foundation for all of the other dreaming practices. It is the first step. Incubation builds the bridge connecting the conscious, unconscious, and higher conscious minds.

Successfully Incubating Dreams

The key to being successful with incubation is practicing it consistently over a period of time. We start by choosing an issue to incubate before we go to sleep. As an example, let's say we have been spending too much time in our head and we want to be more creative and use more of our non-dominant hemisphere. We would ask the following, "Unconscious mind, tonight while I sleep soundly and dream, please assist me in bringing together all of my internal resources so that I am creative and utilize all of my artistic and intuitive abilities." Then we go to sleep and allow our unconscious mind to dream.

When we wake up, anything that we recall from the dream state will apply in some way to the issue which we incubated. We might receive a very direct message in a dream about how we can be more creative, and that is our answer. Another possibility is that we may have a dream which seems totally unrelated so we use the interpretation system in chapter 5 to decipher its message relative to creativity. The most important thing is that if we do not get the answer immediately then we need to consistently keep asking until we do. Oftentimes the unconscious mind wants to see our commitment before providing its deeper responses. If, after a period of time, we still do not get a response, we can then incubate a dream about not getting what we want, so we can find out what is going on! Incubation can be used for any question or issue.

One way to think about how the Universe works is that it is **reflective and facilitative**. This means that it has no stake one way or the other in our desires, needs, or aspirations. It merely maintains whatever momentum we generate. It will not create the momentum for us. That is our job. However, once the momentum is created through consistent and congruent intention, the Universe will maintain the momentum even though we may have moved on to another project. Since we have been consistent, it now needs less frequent attention. Nature can take its course.

Incubating Dream Recall

Almost all dream research suggests that the most important factor in dream recall is...guess what?...**Intention**. It is a striking commentary that the word "intention" is used by dream researchers, who are often hard-core neuroscientists, as the most important variable in dream recall. This fact was discovered serendipitously when researchers noticed that subjects in dream laboratory studies reported more dreams in the laboratory setting than at home. It is as if the subjects' unconscious minds realized they were serious about the dream because they were willing to commit themselves to sleeping in a laboratory!

The number of dreams recalled increases significantly when we intend or structure our life around some aspect of dreaming. In fact, just taking the time to read this book (dream), carry it around, think about it, not to mention putting it under the pillow, will ***increase dream recall***. Again our reading of this is that we are consciously intending something that is important to us. This is a communication to the unconscious and higher conscious minds which will, over time, increase alignment.

One of the easiest ways to remember more dreams is to keep a dream journal. Keeping it on the bedside table or near the bed serves as a symbol, or reminder, of the dreamtime practices. This is a standard technique which will increase recall dramatically. Almost all researchers recommend a dream journal to increase dream recall. If you spontaneously remember an average of at least two dreams per night, a dream journal, for the purpose of achieving lucidity, is optional. Stephen LaBerge, in his studies of lucidity, has determined that those who eventually become skillful lucid dreamers remember at least two dreams per night.

Suggestions to increase dream recall:

1. Keep a dream journal
2. Get adequate rest and sleep
3. Include sufficient amounts of vitamin B6 in your diet
4. Start each day with the Breakfast of Masters
5. Use the incubation technique from this chapter

By following these suggestions, we build our intention and energy to progress in dreaming practices. These are all things that we do during our waking state to pierce through or bridge the "barriers" of sleep. **Sleep is the state which separates our waking lives from our dreaming lives**. The mechanism underlying this "barrier," or threshold, is amnesia. Amnesia is a state of forgetting. Forgetting occurs because of state-dependent learning, which means that what we learn or experience in a particular state is best remembered in that particular state. Generally speaking, the greater the difference between states of consciousness, the greater the chance for amnesia. In cases of radically different states, what happens in one state does not necessarily transfer to the other state and become available for conscious recall, unless there is a method for the transfer to occur. Science recognizes only three special states (waking, sleeping, and dreaming) when this transfer occurs. Hypnosis and meditation are not recognized as separate states, although we believe they are.

There are many day-to-day examples of state-dependent learning. When we used to see clients in our private practice, we would rarely refer to our notes to remember what we had done the previous session. We were in our "professional therapist" state. All we needed to do was sit in our chair in our office with the client in front of us and we would remember all the essentials. However, if you were to ask us about a client while we were shopping, it would take additional time to remember the details. **Information is contextualized in the state where it is needed**. If there is no compelling reason for the information to pass through the threshold, it will not happen.

Practitioners of hypnosis realize that amnesia can occur spontaneously, without suggestion, if the trance state is profound. Amnesia occurs in a very dramatic way for those people who do not remember their dreams while in the waking state. This changes as we begin to build bridges between the waking state and the dreaming state. Once the bridge is in place, we may begin to remember dream sequences spontaneously throughout the course of the day.

Another interesting phenomenon that can occur spontaneously, and which increases as we continue our dreaming practices, is remembering other dreams while we are in a dream. This is not lucidity. While we can do this when we are lucid, we regard this recall as a precursor to lucid dreaming. We begin to remember our dream lives, the parallel lives we live each night as we dream. Instead of experiencing them as isolated, dissociated events of the night, we begin to experience continuity between day and night. It is similar to the way we think about our waking memories, but may not be organized in such a linear way. It is exhilarating to awaken from sleep and remember the continuity of our night dream existence because **no matter what you think you are, you are always more than that**!

Experiences of remembering our dream existence is another indication that we are lifting the veil, or "maya" as the Hindus call it. **Maya is the dream we dream when we are awake—the dream that this is all there is**. In some disciplines from the Far East they would use radical means to assist people in breaking through the two worlds. Some Zen masters would use switches made from trees, others would use a cold plunge, or freezing conditions, to awaken the students to the deeper reality of their existence.

Fasting, sleep deprivation, and intense physical exertion are other ways that are used by Tibetan Buddhists. These techniques were used to break through the barriers between life and death, crossing over into the Void with consciousness.

Often something which is intense, abrupt, and startling will create a breakthrough experience. For the average person the dreams which are most easily remembered are those containing exceptionally heightened emotions and/or bizarre events. These dreams are strong enough to pierce through the amnesia which exists between the sleeping and the waking states. They are getting a message in no uncertain terms from the Higher Self through the unconscious mind. We believe that if we give our dreams the attention they deserve, on an ongoing basis, they will speak to us in a normal speaking voice as opposed to a cryptic whisper or a threatening scream—although the latter adds spice to our dream life! Incubation is the way to begin this dialogue.

The Incubation Process

You can use the following incubation procedure for many different things such as: dream recall, creativity and problem-solving, self-therapy and personal development. Depending on your outcomes for doing incubation, you may or may not need to remember anything about your dreams. It is certainly possible that you may give your unconscious mind a task to do during dreaming that requires no conscious recall on your part. This is similar to using hypnosis and doing everything at the unconscious level so the outcome only becomes evident to the conscious mind over time. You can use dream incubation with the intent of affecting the content of dreams, or for creating outcomes in the waking state, or for creating specific outcomes inside the dream state.

Of course, incubation is an excellent aid to dream recall and eventual lucidity. In Castaneda's apprenticeship, don Juan didn't have Carlos doing "therapy" in his dreams. He initially told Carlos to begin by seeing his hands in his dreams. This is incubating specific content for the dream state that would lead to lucidity. Don Juan also instructed Carlos to find a "power spot" in the desert in his waking state. He was then to find that same spot, or recreate it, as the backdrop of a dream. This is a powerful metaphor for creating a power spot through the process of incubation. It creates the overall backdrop, or context, for the dream content so that whatever occurs is influenced by the personal resources associated with the power spot.

Dream incubation was used widely in ancient and modern Hawaii. Certain kahunas, or healers, would not treat anyone without first incubating a dream or series of dreams. They would begin by seeing the client to gather information, and before they would prescribe anything or carry out any type of healing, they would incubate a dream. The client would then return after the healer had received an answer about what to do with them. The kahunas routinely used dream incubation for answers to guide their healing work

I used this idea when I was doing Wellness seminars for colleges in our area. I wanted to have something interesting to begin my presentation, a story or an anecdote that would add some punch. I gave my unconscious mind the suggestion, "While I sleep soundly and dream, please develop a creative way to open this presentation." I would usually start doing this about a week before the actual presentation. I was always curious about when I would become consciously aware of the information which my unconscious had prepared. Sometimes I did not know what it was until I walked in the door of the auditorium. Once or twice my conscious mind became aware of the story I was going to use while driving to the seminar. I do not remember any occasions when I received the response three or four days ahead of time, because my unconscious mind knew when the deadline was and it knew I did not really need it until then!

The Technique

1. **Decide upon the purpose of the dream**. Formulate the purpose into a "positive internal representation" (an internal picture or pictures, sounds, or words which clearly describe what you want as opposed to what you do not want) and state it as a suggestion which is ***easy to remember*** and to repeat.

   Example: ***"Unconscious mind,*** *tonight while I* ***sleep soundly and dream, please assist me in***...[positive internal representation]."

   "Unconscious mind, *tonight while I* ***sleep soundly and dream, please assist me to heal my body."***

   "Unconscious mind, *tonight while I* ***sleep soundly and dream, please assist me by giving me the most interesting and creative opening for my speech tomorrow morning."***

   The positive internal representation of your purpose ought to be as vivid and compelling as possible, with positive feelings attached to it. It can be stated in general or specific terms, although we prefer to be fairly general when we do this.

2. **Go into peripheral vision (see Dreamtime Interlude 6) and then close your eyes while maintaining the feeling of peripheral vision**. This state has certain parallels with the dream state which increase the likelihood that the suggestion will be "filed" in the same state where it will occur.

3. **While in the closed-eye, peripheral-vision state, repeat the suggestion**. Do this several times during the day and just before you go to bed.

4. **Thank your unconscious and higher conscious minds for helping you as soon as you awaken**. ***Do this*** even if you have received no obvious message or indication that your suggestion was carried out. ***Act*** *as if the* ***suggestion*** *has been carried* ***out.***

In lieu of carrying out the procedure in this format, **another option would be to induce trance**. Using hypnosis, we would induce trance and suggest all of the above while the client was in that state. We have used this procedure as a standard way to complete sessions, especially if the changework was not a hundred percent complete. We would induce trance or simply ask the client to close her eyes and give the suggestion. Sometimes we would even write the suggestion down, like a doctor writes down a prescription, and give it to her to read each night. This is a very effective technique.

In the instructions we would ask the client to repeat the following: "***Unconscious mind, tonight*** *while I* ***sleep soundly and dream,*** *please assist me in* ***mobilizing*** *all my* ***resources*** *so I can* ***achieve my outcome*** *in therapy, so that I can have a productive week and address these issues fully the next session.*" Please refer to *Training Trances* for further discussion of therapeutic dreamwork.

Conscious Review Of Chapter 4

1. **The fundamental distinctions between "enlightened Masters" and everyone else can be summed up in these three areas: intention, energy and the "ego meter."** While there are many other distinctions which could be made, these are the ones that are most important in the development of dreaming practices.

2. **The ideal is for intention to be so one-pointed that we do not have to make distinctions between our conscious, unconscious, and higher conscious minds**. If we collapse the distinctions, the relationship of the three minds is no longer cybernetic, it is simultaneous and one-pointed.

3. **The guiding principle in this ancient system is the question, "Will this raise or lower my energy?"** Everything we do has the potential to influence our energy level—what we eat, where we work, with whom we socialize, and so on.

4. **An enlightened master acknowledges that, "I am more than I think I am" and "I am really not the one doing it anyway."** Otherwise, we limit our actions to only what we conceive ourselves to be—our ego.

5. **Dream incubation is the process of consciously intending the type or function of a dream you want to have, before you actually have it**. It is the foundation for all of the other dreaming practices because it builds the bridge connecting the conscious, unconscious, and higher conscious minds.

6. **One of the easiest ways to remember more dreams is to use a dream journal**. Keeping it on the bedside table or near the bed serves as a symbol, or reminder, of the dreamtime practices.

7. **The experiences of remembering our dream existence is another indication that we are lifting the veil, "maya" as the Hindus call it.** "Maya" is the dream we dream when we are awake—the dream that this is all there is.

8. **You can use the dream incubation procedure for many different things**. Dream recall, creativity, and problem solving skills can all be enhanced through dream incubation. Self-therapy and personal development are also possible.

Unconscious Review Of Chapter 4

Here is an example of a basic, "no frills" incubation induction from a Dream Weekend. Notice that the actual incubation occurs inside of the Dream Meditation Technique (see Dreamtime Interlude 6).

Incubation Double Induction Demonstration

John: So if you would just go ahead and let your body *find a comfortable position*...and when you are ready, just go ahead and begin to let it *relax*.

Julie: That is right, just go ahead and look at a point out in front of you, above eye level. And then as you do, first of all just ***allow your eyes to soften*** while you are looking at that point. Let your muscles relax...

John: And begin ***expanding your awareness***...

Julie: Eye muscles, facial muscles can just relax...

John: Around to the side, even the space...

Julie: Spreading down into your neck...

John: Behind you...

Julie: Perhaps even your shoulders...all the while you can focus your gaze right on that point...

John: Then, when you are ready, ***putting the source of your awareness on your pineal gland, three inches down from the top of your head***...

Julie: ***A few inches behind your third eye***...and just allow your focus to rest there and you can do that with your eyes open or you can just close them, whichever way is easiest for you to have your awareness behind your eyes ...perceiving the world around you...

John: And then, when you are ready, ***put the source of your attention all the way up, eighteen inches above the top of your head and slightly behind it***...

Julie: Notice there is still that image there...

John: All the while maintaining...

Julie: Perhaps of the sun or a flower...

John: Your awareness...

Julie: Or maybe another image of something entirely similar...

John: Expanding...all the way out...

Julie: Or different from any of those that have been suggested so that you can just mark out in space...where exactly...your awareness...would rest...above...your head...

John: Then, if you would, go ahead and ***make your suggestion***...

Julie: Along the lines of...***unconscious mind***...

John: ***Tonight while I sleep soundly and dream***...

Julie: ***Please assist me*** in...

John: All the while keeping your awareness...the source of your awareness...

Julie: Way up above, way up...

John: Source of your awareness...

Julie: Way up...up and behind comfortably, safely...and if you would, just go ahead now and repeat that suggestion several times to your unconscious mind...***unconscious mind, tonight while I sleep soundly and dream, please assist me***...in...to...whatever it is...

John: And then, ***bringing your awareness back into your head,*** the source of your awareness...

Julie: ***Just allow your awareness to just kind of float back down until it is two inches behind your third eye, three inches from the top of your head***...

John: Then begin to move around slightly as you open your eyes but maintain peripheral vision...and then come on back out the whole way. Welcome back!

Chapter 5

Interpreting Dreaming Realities:
Creating Order From Chaos

Chaos Into Meaning

In chapter 3 we discussed the belief that we dream to create. Through dreaming we bring things into existence. Have you ever wondered, once something is created, what lies beyond creation? This is a realm beyond which our conscious and unconscious minds can conceive. It is a realm best described by mystics and quantum physicists. It is a realm known only to our higher conscious mind. What lies beyond our knowable universe? And if we discover that, what is beyond that...and what is beyond that...? And what does that have to do with dream interpretation?

Mathematicians and quantum physicists postulate that chaos is beyond our knowable universe. They use the term "chaos" to denote ambiguity, uncertainty, and that which is beyond the comprehension of our current reality constructs. Very frequently in therapy clients who make big changes ask, "Am I done with this? Does this mean I will never have this problem or anything like it ever again in my life? Can I be **certain**?" These are good questions without easy answers. Yes, at a certain level they are done with that problem and because they have changed, their consciousness has expanded. **However, the same uncertainty that made the change possible will always be there, just beyond our "map" of reality**. When consciousness expands a number of things may happen—particularly experiences that have never been experienced before, both pleasant and not so pleasant.

A Metaphor

Imagine, if you will, that you are climbing a mountain. It is a mountain that you have seen before, in the distance—a huge mountain rising up beyond tall evergreens that are dwarfed by its majesty. You stand on the ground beneath the trees seeing only their rugged, furrowed trunks with the vines that lattice them. The bushes and the tall grass, brown and green, are packed between boulders that were once the mountain. Being among the trees, it is hard to see the forest. You want to see more, so you start the climb. You may have imagined for a long time how awesome it would be to climb this mountain to see what you could see, and now you are doing it.

After a while you look down at the area where you began, and you can see all the other fields, forests, valleys, and mountains that are visible only from this vantage point. Gone are the rough trunks and vines and the patterns they formed. Gone is the boulder that was once the ground on which you stood. You also notice, to your surprise, that the forest you were in extends much further than you thought. "So it is a big forest," you think to yourself.

You climb another several thousand feet and look down at where you were. At first you cannot find the "big" forest sandwiched between two massive forests bordered by wide golden fields of grain. It seems so small. You think, "I guess it is not so big after all." As you continue your climb, you tire and begin thinking, "This mountain is a hell of a lot taller than I thought, and steeper, too." Eventually you get to the top and marvel at the vista. You can see so much more than before...the evergreen forest, the others beside it...a granite, snow-topped giant of a mountain which makes the one you are on seem like rolling farmland...the junkyard filled with rusted cars heaped in disheveled piles...the brownish-yellow pollution hanging in the air above the tall grey buildings you can now see in the distance...the crystal blue river carving its way though the valley whose banks are dotted with farms and small villages...meeting the azure sky on the horizon.

As night falls you look back at the city. You no longer see the pollution but instead, the twinkling lights of activity, the lighted grids formed by the streets that lead out in all directions, and the junkyard that has receded into the night shadowed by the tall trees. You also see the river whose presence is only known by the reflection of the stars and the moon in the purple black night. All of these things you could never have seen at the bottom: the beauty and the ugliness. Chaos and the order. The seen and the unseen. The change. But you are filled with the experience. You cannot put it into words. It changes you. When you go back down to the bottom, the forest will never be quite the same; neither will you, and that is good.

A Change In Meaning Is A Change In Consciousness

For us life is a continuous folding of chaos into order and order into chaos. One of the primary findings of the science of chaos is that chaos is "enfolded into" (recedes into) order, but even deeper, another chaos takes over with an even deeper order behind that. According to the late physicist David Bohm, there is no irreducible randomness. When we study only the explicate order (our material world), structure seems to arise from chaos. This, however, is only an abstraction of a more encompassing order. What appear to be chance events or anomalies, such as spontaneous healing, actually reveal a pattern of the superorder in which these events are embedded. Each event, or electron, is "aware" or knows the overall plan in which it participates! On a quantum level, meaning arises from the interaction of the electron with its field. The information field acts on the particle and gives it "guidance." Does this sound anything like our connection to our higher conscious mind?

Based on Bohm's model, meaning can be enfolded (recede into) and unfolded at (emerge from) multiple levels. Therefore that meaning is an infinite, unending range of consciousness. It is never complete. When we find a discrepancy on one level, it will always be clarified by expanding the context. The bottom line is that the higher levels will always be characterized by ambiguity.

When we periodically experience chaos in our lives it means we are ascending. It means that there will be a point in the future where we will once again feel the security of certainty. The trick is to allow ourselves to experience the chaos long enough to allow the new order to emerge. All too often we try to eliminate uncertainty even at the risk of knowing something before it is ready to be unfolded. It takes patience, trust, and plain old good judgement to experience the chaos before it is ready to create a higher order.

For most of us there is no better example of the chaos of creation than our dreams. Learning to interpret our dreams and learning the language of our unconscious symbols is one way to create meaning from chaos. Remember that a change in meaning is a change in consciousness. As suggested in Alfred Korzybski's landmark work *Science And Sanity* (1933), "**all meaning is context-dependent**." One of the ways to change meaning is to change context. Anything we define as a "problem" is related to the context, or the "box," in which we place it. Most of us at various times have experienced contradictions, inconsistencies, and paradoxes in our lives, particularly in our dreams. The way to dissolve contradictions, inconsistencies, and paradoxes is by broadening our context. To widen our context, or extend our metaphors, we have to be willing to experience the temporary chaos of new information, even though it may not seem to fit the "box" or metaphor which we have used to describe our reality.

Our dreams can assist us in accessing information from higher realms. Our job is to integrate the information we get from higher realms and ground it in our physical reality. How can we hold the "truth" of our dreams on one hand, and the "truth" of our waking reality on the other hand, and bring them together to form a higher truth that includes both and resolves inconsistencies, contractions, and paradoxes? To understand this, we will now explore how we can use our dreams to change our consciousness.

The Dreamind Triangle Interpretation System

This system of interpretation is a hybrid developed from our exploration of other dream systems. In our system there are no universal archetypes, or symbols, for dream interpretation. Sorry, there is no dream dictionary either! Why not? Because our view, which is a departure from the normal one, is that **the only one who can know the meaning of the symbols is the person who has the dream**. Dreams are symbolic representations created by the unconscious mind. They are messages created in individual codes. If we offer an interpretation it is only that: our *interpretation* of the dream. How could we possibly know the full extent of someone else's unconscious symbology and be certain that *our* interpretation is accurate?

Here is an example. I remember years ago learning that water in dreams was a universal symbol for "mother." How was that decided? Is it possible that it was someone else's (Jung's, perhaps!) interpretation of water? I had a dream with water in it (which we will discuss later in this chapter) and my symbolic interpretation was "openness," and not mother. In this same dream, I saw the faces of the three commentators for *Monday Night Football*. I do not even watch *Monday Night Football*! If I did not have this system, I might have been tempted to run out to my local bookstore, find a dream dictionary, and discover what significance this had for me. And if they did not include this as a dream symbol, then what would I do? Our position is a radical departure from most of the previous literature about dreams. We believe that ultimately the only person who can interpret your dreams is you. **This means that everyone is responsible for his/her own dream interpretation.**

We should note here that in many of the systems of the cultures which we have studied, dream interpretation was not carried out in this way. While our system differs from these, we have great respect for these cultures and the ways in which they interpret dreams. Unfortunately, the Western world does not have some of the advantages that these cultures enjoy, so we have created something which works within our own time-space coordinates.

The Hawaiian System

One culture in which we have taken a personal interest is that of Hawaii. In the Hawaiian system someone known as a *kahuna wehe wehe* (a dream unraveller) determines the meaning of dreams. The Hawaiian system by its very nature has built-in safeguards. Dream interpretation, like many other special skills, is set up through the *ohana* (the extended family). Each family has its own *kahuna wehe wehe*, a family member designated before, or within a few years after, their birth to be the family's dream interpreter. This person is in an excellent position to interpret symbols because he/she knows the family history and its issues, as well as the dreams of several living generations of family members. The *kahuna wehe wehe* learns about the previous generations from an elder who is the keeper of this information. Because they pass this information down for so many generations, they have very accurate information about the archetypes and symbols for their particular family.

The Yogic System

In the Hindu system a guru often interprets the dreams of the disciples. Certainly, as people develop, this may be necessary. In the long term, however, most gurus do not let this become a habit, as **the philosophy of the yogic system is to know oneself**. This is a system designed to create self-reliance, and the ultimate idea is for the disciple to be unified within. Gurus serve their disciples by leading them to their inner god or goodness. We agree with this and believe that by interpreting our own dreams we can get to know and understand our deeper nature. It is in this spirit that we created this system.

Research Findings And Conclusions

Teaching others how to interpret their own personal symbology is also consistent with the latest in research findings (Hobson, 1988). One of the important theories of dream creation, discussed in chapter 3, is that **dreams are our attempt to make sense of the random chemical firings occurring in the brain**. The dream content, and later the meaning, is our mind's way of assimilating those random firings. In this sense, the random firings which we experience are quite different from those experienced by our parents, lovers, therapists, or dream dictionary authors!

The purpose of any dream practice—whether it is incubation, interpretation, completion, or lucidity—is to create alignment among the conscious, unconscious, and higher conscious minds. The purpose of dreaming is to receive messages from our higher conscious minds. One of the ways in which our higher conscious mind connects with us and guides us is through our dream life. **Dreams are messages from the higher conscious mind. To understand these messages we need to know how to interpret them.**

Overview Of The Process

In this process, each of the three minds plays a particular role. The higher conscious mind—the spirit inside us which is plugged into the universal intelligence—sends the message. The unconscious mind provides the arena, the backdrop, the content, and the symbols for the message. The conscious mind then receives, analyzes and interprets the symbols and content. These three aspects of our mind work together to bring inner alignment and harmony.

We have summarized this below in the form of the "**Dreamind Triangle**."

Higher conscious mind
sends message

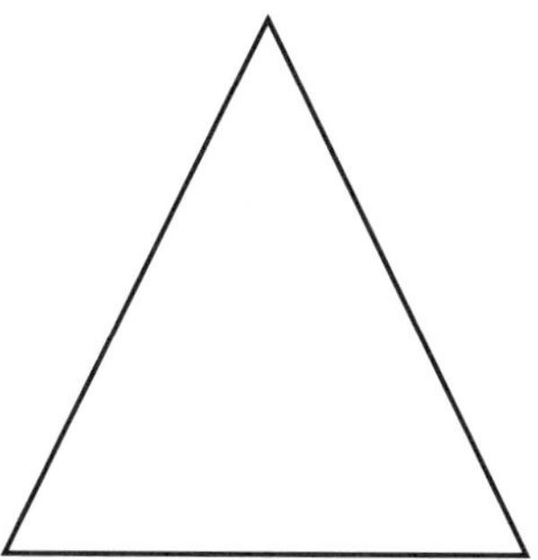

Unconscious mind
encodes message

Conscious mind
interprets message

Using this triangle, you begin this process by listing the elements of your dream under the section for the unconscious mind. You then determine the abstract meaning of each element and list it under the section for the conscious mind. This set of associations is then used to guide you to the message from the higher conscious mind. The process is completed with a word or phrase which signifies the action which needs to be taken.

Demonstration

Context: Julie carried out a dream incubation the night before teaching this material as preparation for the workshop.

Dream (unconscious mind section):

- John and I are in a small wooden boat on some kind of water
- there are people in the boat but I cannot see their faces
- at a certain point it seems really crowded
- all of a sudden there are these three faces that appear
- they are the three guys from *Monday Night Football* and they do not say anything
- scene changes suddenly
- now I am on the top deck of a cruise ship
- everywhere, people are enjoying themselves
- the mood is very joyful
- I take a towel and sit down beside the swimming pool
- as I do, the swimming pool changes color to this gorgeous silver blue
- the water begins to swirl and suddenly the water comes right out of the swimming pool and goes out into the ocean.
- then it ends

Unconscious (dream)	**Conscious (association)**
John and I	Together
Small, wooden boat	Being stuck, earth-bound
Water	Openness
People—cannot see faces	Transparent, spirits
Crowded	Bogged down
Three faces—*Monday Night Football*	Three selves
They do not say anything	Quiet but solid
Sudden scene change	Fast, quick movement
Top deck of a cruise ship	Something big and easy is happening
People everywhere	Love everywhere
People enjoying themselves	Having fun, happiness
Towel	Security

Sitting down by the swimming pool	Cleansing
Water in the pool changes color, starts to swirl, and goes into the ocean	Awesome transformation
Then it ends	It has begun

Context for interpretation: This dream may be interpreted as:

a) an incubation request relative to the dream workshop, or
b) a message relating to Julie's personal life. She chose the latter.

Conscious (association)	**Higher conscious (message)**
Together	How I want to be
Being stuck, earth-bound	A turnoff
Openness	Being part of everything
Transparent, spirits	Spirit is my real nature
Bogged down	Pressure, obligations
Three selves	Need to better integrate my three selves to resolve issue
Quiet, but solid	State I need to be inside
Fast, quick movement	The change will be quick
Something big and easy is happening	I am ready to move up a level
Love everywhere, fun, happiness	This is how I will feel
Security	I have the strength to do it
Cleansing	Forgiving myself for not being perfect
Awesome transformation	I probably did not realize I could get to this level
It has begun	I did not know consciously how much was happening

Overall message: (Stated verbatim) "Sometimes life is a turnoff because there is too much pressure and it gets in the way. However, I can cleanse that. I will be successful at resolving this by being solid and quiet, and that will move me on to the next level.

When I integrate the whole thing, then something big will occur which will make a transformational change in my life. There is really something very positive happening and when I increase rapport with my three selves, I can really make a fantastic change.

"There is still a conflict between earth and spirit inside me that needs to be resolved. It is a parts conflict between materialism and doing what I have to do in life, and being free to be a free spirit. The way to resolve it is by being in deeper rapport with my higher conscious mind, my unconscious mind, and my conscious mind and by being silent and still. The message I would put in the triangle is **stay silent and still**."

Now, if we were using this as a therapeutic intervention, we would ask her, "What is stopping you right now from resolving this and being the way you want to be?" We would take whatever answer she gave us and use the **Unconscious Interviewing For Clearing Technique** (see Dreamtime Interlude 4, as well as **Getting To Know Your Higher Conscious Mind**, Dreamtime Interlude 5). Alternatively, if she wanted to continue with some nightly therapy of her own, she could incubate another dream and ask her higher conscious mind what to do next. A suggestion for incubation may sound like this: "Tonight, while I sleep soundly and dream, please assist me in utilizing all of my resources to make the changes which need to occur on the inside, so that I can be silent and still in my everyday life."

Using dream incubation, unconscious interviewing, clearing, and interpretation interchangeably reinforces dreamtime practices as a personal development system. The individual has maximum control and freedom regarding personal changes, with the safeguard that the unconscious mind and higher conscious mind will only go as far as the person's resources allow If the above demonstration had occurred as part of a therapeutic relationship, we would suggest that the client use incubation, and we would also carry out some of changework during the session. The changework we would elect to carry out at this point would be a parts integration between "earth" and "spirit."

Since dreams are, in our opinion, holographic, then we can expect the conflict in the above demonstration to also be representative of other areas in the subject's life, such as career, relationships, and family. In the same way, all the other issues in her life become a reflection of this parts conflict represented in her personal life. **Change on one level will lead to change on the other levels because of the holographic nature of life.**

The Technique (See Dreamind Triangle Diagram)

1. **Write down the dream as you remember it in words or brief phrases under the unconscious mind section of the triangle.** To recall it, you may find it helpful to lie down and close your eyes for a while, then open your eyes to write down the phrases that describe the contents of the dream. (It does not matter how much content you recall—just be honest.)

2. **Look at each of these words or phrases in turn and write down your association for each under the conscious mind section of the triangle.**
   a) Go into peripheral vision (see Dreamtime Interlude 6).
   b) Ask, "What does ... mean to me?"
   c) Go with your first association even if it does not make sense to you. (In many cases, as you are starting out, it will not make logical sense.)
   d) Write down your associations verbatim.

3. **Look at all the associations elicited in step 2 and ask, "To what issue in my life right now do all of these relate?" Write your response in the context/question box.** What is the real context of this dream? Answering this question will provide the life context to which it applies.

4. **Look at each association listed under the conscious mind section while asking, "How does ... relate to the issue I just wrote in the context box, or to my life in general?"** Go with your first response and write the answer for each association near the top of the triangle, marked higher conscious mind. If you have incubated a dream, then ask, "How does this [association] relate to [question or issue from the dream incubation]?"

5. **Write or draw the overall spirit of the message in the center of the triangle.**

6. **Look at the entire triangle going back and forth between foveal and peripheral vision** (see Dreamtime Interlude 6). This tends to further facilitate integration by having you observe different levels of reality simultaneously.

7. **Put the message into action**. The degree to which you implement the message in your life is a good indicator of the degree of your inner alignment regarding this issue.

To use this system of interpretation, you use whatever you remember from your dream, even if you think it is just a small amount. Over the years many people have told us they "never remember" their dreams. Our view is that you remember what is important to remember. Even if it is a dreamlet or brief vignette, that is fine. Sometimes this makes it easier to interpret because you have less content with which to work. It is like reading a dictionary: you do not have to read the whole book to find out the meaning of one word. You just go directly to the location of the word. Your unconscious and higher conscious minds know how to do that for you. It is as if they are saying, "You could read the whole dictionary if you want to (in fact you have, when you dreamed the whole dream) and if you want to know the essence, here it is. Just remember this part and you will be fine."

Make sure you write down the words exactly as they come up. Do not edit or reframe them. When doing this with another person, repeat what they tell you to make sure you understood. Repeating their words back to them stimulates the neural networks inside their body relative to this issue. This tends to create a more powerful effect when the interpretation unravels. Write down phrases exactly as they say them, using their pauses to distinguish one phrase from another.

The associations which are listed under the conscious mind need to be abstract. They need to be of a higher logical level than the dream phrases. For example, if "mountain" is a dream word, then "challenge" might be its abstract equivalent listed under the conscious mind section.

When you decide upon the context in which to interpret the dream you can ask any question. You can use one dream to look at each level of your life because everything in life is set up holographically. Similar patterns will be present across the contexts in your life. In this way, each area of your life is a microcosm of your life in general. Everything is a reflection of everything else. It does not really matter which context you pick because they are all holographic representations of one another. Also, we are meaning-making organisms. Our conscious and unconscious minds construct meaning in every situation. One of our positions is that every dream we have is just a metaphor for our life. It is no accident if, for example, a person has a dream about running up a hill—the chances are that this metaphor has significance in more than one context of his/her life.

A positive by-product of the interpretation is that eventually we recognise and understand the language and symbols of our unconscious mind. For example, I have learned that, for me, climbing is a symbol for spiritual growth, or "ascension." An interesting thing happens as a result of how we construct our realities. We **start to notice these dream symbols crossing over into our waking reality**. Many times they are symbols for the same thing in waking reality and in dreams.

Julie was carrying out a dream interpretation with me (John). A prominent part of the dream was that I was walking through the front door of our home, looking at our staircase and then walking up it. For me, this meant moving to a higher spiritual level, which I had never before equated with walking up steps. A couple of weeks after this, I was cycling up a very steep hill in Hawaii. Later, someone who had seen me doing this asked what I liked about riding. I said I really enjoyed riding up hills. At the time I thought this was a little weird! That is when I got the BFO (blinding flash of the obvious). Riding up hills is a concrete metaphor for moving up to higher levels. **Our personal symbols are *our* personal symbols**, whether they apply to our dream reality or our waking reality.

When you receive the message from your higher conscious mind, you move from the abstract to the specific. The more specific the question you ask, the more specific the information you receive will be. While looking at all of these specifics, you consider what action you need to take to follow through with the message. **The information from the Higher Self needs to be grounded on the physical level**. This is the critical point which brings alignment to all three minds. It brings the process full circle. The higher conscious mind begins by sending a coded message through the unconscious mind to the conscious mind. The conscious mind then consults with the unconscious mind to determine the meaning of the symbols. Consultation helps you to get to the specifics of the message. In the final phase, it is up to the conscious mind to act (or not) on the message. This is ultimately how to develop rapport between the higher conscious mind and the conscious mind. **If you follow through with action, the higher conscious mind recognizes that its information is being taken seriously**.

After the action has been decided upon, **the entire dream process is summarized by a word or phrase**. This may occur spontaneously during the action phase. One particular word might feel more meaningful to you than others. Sometimes the word comes before the action, as they generally occur around the same time in the process. This word or phrase is then written in the middle of the triangle. Focus on this word or phrase in foveal vision, then in peripheral vision, and continue alternating back and forth. This activates and consolidates all the neural networks associated with this dream process. You are creating a gestalt, or a complete representation of the process, which is summarized in one word or phrase.

Another way to utilize dream interpretation is to ask yourself a question (just as in incubation) and have a dream partner who dreams the dream for you. Before they go to sleep, they have the intention of having "your" dream. Don't tell them the question that their dream is the answer to so that their conscious mind does not become involved with the unconscious process. After they have had the dream, ask them to tell you exactly what happened in it. Write down their dream verbatim. Then use the Dreamind Triangle Interpretation System to interpret it just as if it was your dream. Because on one level, it was!

If you use this system, it does not really matter what you use as the object of the interpretation. You could pick a rock and notice its contour and shape. List these observations and then interpret them in the same way you did the Dreamind process. This was also done with clouds in ancient cultures. Today, in terms of psychology, we refer to it as a Rorschach test, which is based upon the notion that perception is projection. **The value of doing this with your dreams is that there is a more obvious connection between your dreams and your higher conscious mind.**

The Dreamind Triangle Interpretation System

Context Question —>

Higher conscious mind
sends message

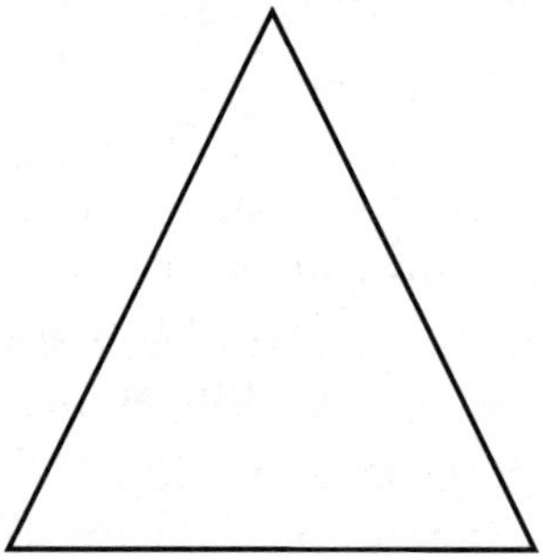

Unconscious mind
encodes message

Conscious mind
interprets message

Action:

Dreams Which Need No Interpretation

There are some dreams that need little or no effort to interpret. Often premonition dreams are like this. In Hawaii they are called *Ho ike na ka po* which means "**revelations of the night, an Aumakua, or Higher Self-advised dream.**" In these dreams our unconscious and higher conscious minds collude and say, "Look, we really do not need to code this one; he is ready for it, just give it to him." We wake and instantly know what the dream is about. We know what is going to happen. There is no guesswork involved. We know it like we know the back of our hand.

In an interview with a Hawaiian expert on dreams, he told us of one premonition dream in his family. His mother dreamed that one of her sons was driving on the freeway and was hurt very badly. She had to *oki* (cut) the dream. He explained that while *oki* means "to cut," it does not mean "to cut" in the way the Western mind would understand it. *Oki* would occur only through *pule* (prayer). The mother prayed intently for several days. A number of days passed and the son was involved in a car accident on the freeway, but sustained only minor injuries. As far as the mother was concerned, she had actually intervened on his behalf. She believed she was given her dream so that she could intervene to protect him.

Here is an experience that preceded a dream I had some time ago. It is a little graphic and personal. It is also a good example of having lots of symbols and an overriding message which was not only very clear, but prophetic. I found some blood in my stool and was freaked out. Being healthy and physically active, the biggest problems I have ever had have been minor, sports-related injuries. I made an appointment with my family doctor and he scheduled an extensive battery of tests to reassure me. He told me not to worry, that it was probably an irritation or something minor. Unfortunately, because of our schedule, we could not get the most important tests carried out for two weeks. During those two weeks, every fear I have ever had about dying or getting a major illness came up. To make matters worse, I was experiencing congestion in my left side, in my colon.

Just a few days before this, we had completed three weeks of training, and I knew that my eating habits were not as consistent or healthy as they usually were. I immediately cleaned up my diet, and used the whole experience as the impetus to clean up any psychological or emotional issues that may have been remotely related to this. Despite all of my efforts, I was scared. I had an underlying feeling of anxiety.

Fortunately for me, this happened soon after Julie had become a Reiki Master. During the time when I was awaiting the tests, each night we fell asleep, she would do Reiki on my left side, while I was awaiting the tests. Several nights before the tests and after a lot of emotional clearing and Reiki, I had the following dream. This is very close to the form in which I originally wrote it.

The Dream

Walking along a street, I meet a man and woman who are attractive, somewhat older than I, and obviously a couple. They seem to be some kind of guides. They never actually tell me this, and I am surprised in the dream that I even think it! They tell me that they have plans for me and also for Julie—I vaguely remember their saying something to the effect that Julie is here to help me; that they are training her.

Scene change: I end up on what seems to be an operating table. The man and woman and then Julie use some instrument that initially projects lightning and then they start pulling something out of me, from my abdominal area. It does not hurt. I am sort of in a state of suspension, half scared, half awestruck. They start to pull something out of me that is white and it looks like part of my intestinal tract. It is very white, clean, and luminescent. It has a tufted appearance. As they do this, lightning arcs from it and then, a little bit later, I wake up. I feel a sense of well-being and am looking forward to getting the tests completed.

I knew this dream was significant. It **felt** really spiritual. These guides—and I do not particularly subscribe to the idea of guides in the New Age sense, when I am in my waking state—really seemed to be here to help me, and were doing so through Julie. I really felt that. I hoped that the dream exorcised anything that might have been inside me. Several days later I had the tests and everything was clear. The picture of my colon I had seen in the dream looked exactly like the one I saw on the computer monitor. Sometimes we are lucky enough to get the direct line from the higher conscious mind. This was one of those times.

Just One Big Dream

In closing, we thought we would share something with you that is one of those "good things to think about." **What if, when we dream, we are all dreaming the same dream**? One big dream. We can demonstrate this from a linguistic point of view. If we take the words in our dreams and continue to move up to higher levels of abstraction, eventually the content and the meaning of everybody's dream is going to end up in the same place. We are all just dreaming that one big dream differently because of the life experiences we have had. It is important to look at our dreams in a way that brings us back to that notion. We are all talking about the same thing but from our own unique perspectives. We are living our own dreams that are really the expressions of this one big dream, with all of its levels of meaning, showing us all the different ways of getting back to where we started: **back to the One**.

Conscious Review Of Chapter 5

1. **Mathematicians and quantum physicists postulate that chaos is beyond our knowable universe**. They use the term "chaos" to denote ambiguity, uncertainty, and that which is beyond the comprehension of our current reality constructs.

2. **Life is a continuous folding of chaos into order and order into chaos**. One of the primary findings of the science of chaos is that chaos is enfolded into (receding into) order, and then another, even deeper chaos takes over with an even deeper order behind that.

3. **The only one who can really know your dream symbols is you**. Your dreams are symbolic representations, created by your unconscious mind, and created in your own individual code. Therefore we are all responsible for our own dream interpretation.

4. **Dreams are messages from the higher conscious mind**. To understand these messages we need to know how to interpret them.

5. **Using dream incubation, unconscious interviewing, clearing, and interpretation reinforces dreamtime practices as a personal development system**. The individual has maximum control regarding personal changes, with the safeguard that the information provided will be in proportion to his/her resourcefulness.

6. **The Dreamind Triangle Interpretation System is used to obtain the message of the dream from the higher conscious mind**. A series of associations and specific questions unlock the meaning of the dream symbols.

7. **Premonition dreams need little effort to interpret**. In these dreams our unconscious and higher conscious minds provide the message very directly so that no interpretation is necessary.

8. **As you stretch your mind, consider this: when we dream what if we are all dreaming the same dream**? What if there is just one big dream and we all dream it differently because of our life experiences?

Unconscious Review Of Chapter 5

As your conscious mind is reading this page we do not know if it is ***most intrigued*** by the notion of chaos enfolding into order or order unfolding into chaos...and perhaps this is not really as important to your conscious mind as it is to ***you're unconscious***...and it is good to know when you are...that is, intrigued by new possibilities...because it really is your unconscious that transforms what seems like chaos into what seems like order, is it not? Only to find a deeper level below both of those that is completely unknowable to the conscious mind...which has inherent limitations...while being exquisitely understood by the...unconscious mind ...at its deepest level.

As you are reading this, it is your conscious mind that is looking at the page and ***you're unconscious*** that is making sense of it. In the same way, it is your unconscious mind that creates your dream symbols as a way of communicating messages to you...while your conscious mind attempts to make sense of them... Who knows how many unconscious dream symbols you may have in a given dream, in a given night, in a given week, in a given year, in a given lifetime? How could we know how many dream symbols you have and what they mean...when they are yours...in your own unique way, aren't they? So go ahead and try not to ask yourself, "What does that particular symbol mean?"...until you no longer ask because you know now...how important those messages can be...especially when you realize that they come as guidance from the higher conscious mind...in order to protect you, guide you, comfort and inspire you to live your dreams to the fullest...and fully enjoy the process of living your dreams...

So when you are ready, go ahead and dream on and on...until the messages from your Higher Self are *so clear* that they lead you to certain actions, behaviors, and insights that change your life only for the better...you are...when you trust the inner alignment of the **three** minds...until you **two** realize they are only **ONE** mind...and this is only ONE BIG DREAM we are all living together...so **rest assured** of that, as you sleep soundly and dream tonight!

Chapter 6

Lucidity:

The Dream That Wakes You Up

Lucid dreaming is the ability to be consciously aware of dreaming while in a dream. It is experienced by most people who remember their dreams, but only infrequently. There are numerous ways to develop this skill. We have explored many of them ourselves. In this chapter, we provide techniques which we have found useful. While there are some who view lucid dreaming as an end in itself, we do not. We see it as another process that can be used to align the conscious, unconscious, and higher conscious minds.

In dream yoga and other systems of enlightenment, lucidity is just the beginning of the entire process of transcendence. It is a means **to transcend the consensual reality in which we live**—the one most of us consider to be the "real" one. Then there is our dream reality. As we have mentioned, most of the time when we are awake we do not question whether something is real or not. We just accept the fact that this reality is real. Now, think about this for a second: how many times when we dream do we ever doubt the reality of the dream? Don't most of us accept whatever happens even if it is totally bizarre? Once we are inside the domain of the dream, it is real. So which reality is more valid than the other? Approximately five years in total of our life is actually spent night-dreaming, so why not view this as an equally valid reality?

A Separate Reality: When We Decided, "It Is Just A Dream."

How did we ever decide that our waking state was the "real" one and the dream state was something other than "real"? Piaget, a well-known child development theorist, studied this question and found that until most of us are approximately four years old we do not make any distinction between dreams and our waking life (LaBerge, 1986). In fact, during our first years of life we dream far more than later in life. So how did we learn to make the distinction? Those of us from the Western world learned the difference between the dream state and the waking state in an archetypical way. Probably one night we were having a scary dream and we woke up. Let us say that we dreamed there was a monster under the bed. Well, before the age of four, if we dreamed that a monster was under the bed, in the waking state we would have the same belief—there was a monster under the bed! What did we do next? We probably rushed over to our parents' room and the following scenario ensued. "There is a monster under my bed! There's a monster under my bed!" "Don't worry, honey, **it was only a dream**. Everything will be okay."

While dreaming, the brain relies on its own internal stimulation rather than external stimulation to create the dreamscape. We create and react to our own inner world which, in many ways, is as rich as, if not richer than, the external world. From a quantum physics point of view, this distinction of "out there" versus "in here" is entirely a product of Newtonian and Cartesian thinking. Now, the normal conduit for our dreams is sleep. The question is how do we expand the conduit so that we have freer access to our waking and dreaming states? Paradoxically, in the reality-test section we said that it is important to create a separation between these states. The reason for this is that it is important to be really clear about what the differences are, so we know what we are bridging. Once the bridges are constructed, we realize that it is not just a waking reality and not just a dream reality, **it is all reality**! Some people refer to this one reality as the **Dreamtime**.

Dreaming Possibilities

There is a whole realm of reality outside our normal awareness. Carlos Castaneda's book, *The Art Of Dreaming* (1993), gives an excellent account of what the new physics (or quantum physics) would call parallel universes—realities which are typically outside of our band of perception. One way to experience these is to have a dream, wake up in it, go back to sleep, have another dream inside a dream, and wake up in that one also. Moving further into these realities is a means for exploring these parallel universes or to parallel levels of existence. **The key to all of this is that you**

need to know how to get back from these realms. Mastering Reality Testing (Dreamtime Interlude 1) and the Dreaming Meditation Technique (Dreamtime Interlude 6) will help you to do this. What we are really talking about here is bridging the gap, so we are taking consciousness into areas where we have not normally directed it before.

In this sense, lucid dreaming models the principle of creation because, when we are dreaming lucidly, we are as close as most of us will ever be to an experience of total, raw creation. There is an open field and then there is a thought. There is consciousness and it focuses on a thought. The more energy that goes into the thought, the more it becomes real. This state is beyond space, time, matter, and cause/effect. Most people do not really report being "a body" in a dream—they experience themselves as consciousness in a formless kind of way.

Being beyond the notion of cause and effect sets up an interesting metaphor of reality. If we can go beyond our normal beliefs in dreams by creating and manifesting things, what will happen when we are really adept at this and we wake up? The same neural connections will be there in the waking state, but they will need to be conditioned to our waking biochemistry through intention and action. Some masters like Castaneda are at the point where they can flip back and forth between the two realities at will.

Once lucidity occurs, there are lots of choices—anything is possible. The usual constraints are lifted. We are no longer leaves blowing in the wind as we are when we dream unconsciously. We now have a conscious choice to create and design our reality. There is a lot of room for exploration. There was a period when I went around visiting artists, musicians, and people from various fields whom I had always thought were creative. This is a useful phase to go through. It provides access to a tremendous amount of information at the neurological and experiential level. We can meet anyone we want in our dreams. Anyone we can think of is a possibility, because we are operating at the level of thought! We could ride a light beam with Einstein, paint with Van Gogh, or write music with Beethoven.

Through lucidity and incubation, one of my most gratifying meetings was with Dr. Milton Erickson, who has been an inspiration of ours for almost fifteen years. Over the course of about a year, I experienced numerous dreams which were extremely instructive and inspiring. Some of these dreams were lucid, some were not.

One series of dreams that was particularly memorable was when I was in "supervision" with Dr. Erickson. In the dream, I was working in a prison as a counselor and Dr. Erickson was my clinical supervisor. On a number of occasions, I actually became lucid when I thought that Dr. Erickson was beginning to hypnotize me as a part of my supervision. At one point I remember asking him, "Are you trying to put me in trance?" I was feeling light-headed and woozy. The quality of my visual field was starting to change. Everything looked like fluid, very watery and shiny. (This shininess is one of my dream signs.) He did not answer my question and, as I waited, I started to float out of my body and looked down on myself in the chair in a dimly lit room with him. At that point, I realized I was in a dream and **consciously** decided to enter the trance he was initiating.

This was a powerful experience for me. I remained lucid for only a short time. It was so gratifying not only to dream of being with Erickson, but to have the conscious awareness of doing so while it was happening! I took with me the feeling that his spirit is still available and present to those who need or want his help. I had consciously lived a "waking dream" that I had never thought possible, as Erickson died in 1980. Some time after I awakened, I wondered whether it was "really" Erickson or just a "figment of my imagination." How could I ever know for sure? Over a period of time I decided that it was a "real" experience and nothing else really mattered. It affected me and I knew it. I do know that in our dreams we are beyond time, space, matter, and energy. If time does not exist, then neither do the concepts of life and death that we understand in our waking reality. **Is it possible that when we dream and are lucid, and even when we are not lucid, we are really contacting the Infinite, the One**? This experience of mine, as well as many others that we will describe, led us to this conclusion. On our "bad" days, we can still be skeptical and deny this interpretation, but we cannot deny the experience.

The Process Of Becoming And The Process Of Becoming Lucid

Developing lucidity skills is very similar to learning how to enter a deep hypnotic trance or falling asleep at night. It is something that we need to intend, although it is largely mediated by unconscious processes. It requires a balance of enthusiasm and patience. If we "try really hard" to become lucid, it is possible that we may not sleep very well. We can put so much pressure on ourselves that we never **relax enough** to fall asleep. We mention this only because it was a phase of our own development in learning to dream lucidly. Either fortunately or unfortunately, we had no formal teacher to whom we could turn for advice. We read lots of books, and talked to lots of people, but largely we had to follow our own instincts and learn by trial and error. It was probably not the fastest path, but we learned a lot about ourselves and dreaming along the way and can pass on a lot of learnings as a result.

Remembering Dreams: Keeping A Dream Journal

To begin lucid dreaming practices, you need to aim to be able to recall at least two dreams per night. If you recall two or more dreams a night, you have enough rapport with your unconscious mind to begin lucid dreaming practices. Otherwise, increasing your recall is the first and most important step. After all, how can you know if you are having lucid dreams if you cannot remember your dreams in the first place! You could be having all of these great lucid dreams yet you would never know it! **Just as with any other part of dream practices or spiritual practices in general, intention is everything**.

The vast majority of research on dream recall suggests that the key to recalling your dreams is to simply have a strong intention to do so. There are two easy ways to structure your intention. The first is to keep a dream journal. Remember, like giving gifts, it is the thought that counts. Find a notebook that you will only use for recording dreams. Do whatever you like to adorn it. Put it next to your bed or even under your pillow.

In the morning, before you do anything else, record your dreams. Record anything, no matter how insignificant or small. The best way to recall your dreams is to move as little as possible when you awaken. The more you move, the more your physiology and biochemistry will change. When you first awaken your biochemistry is the same or very similar to when you dream. Just lie quietly with your eyes closed and let whatever dreams you had come to mind. Stay relaxed. When a dream or dream fragment comes, take a moment to let it register, reach over and get your journal, and then write it down. Most researchers agree that it is best to **record the date and to give the dream a title**. From a neurological perspective this consolidates the dream into a gestalt. We recommend that you entitle the dream only after you have written all that you are going to write about it. **Write the dream in present tense**, as if you are experiencing it as you write. Do not be concerned about the literary nature of your writing, the style, punctuation, or grammar. Just write down whatever comes from the unconscious mind. The most important element to writing down your dreams, particularly if you are going to interpret them, is to **be completely honest about the content**. If, for any reason, it is not comfortable for you to actually put the dream content down in writing, then write those feelings down, as if they were part of the dream. Often it is useful to write down your thoughts which occur upon waking up, particularly if they seem related in any way to the dream.

If you are really committed, **you can set your alarm clock to wake you up after you complete a dream cycle**. We have never done this, but many dream researchers claim that this is the best way to remember your dreams: by writing down dreams from each cycle immediately after the cycle is complete. These same researchers suggest learning to write with your eyes closed or partially closed, while remaining in the position in which you were sleeping. You might ask, "Do I really need to go this far?" You need to go far enough to convince your unconscious that you are serious. Different people will need to do this in different ways. The question is, **"Are you willing to do whatever it takes to remember your dreams?"**

The second way to structure the intention to recall dreams is to incubate recall. Simply use the same incubation method you learned in chapter 4, asking your unconscious mind to assist your conscious mind in recalling your dreams. We can assure you that the more time you spend thinking about, writing about, and reading about dreams during the day, the more you will recall your dreams and the more likely you are to become lucid. This is why people go to ashrams and meditation retreats so they can put virtually one hundred percent of their energy into one specific thing. This brings us to the most important question in the system. **Do you have the time, energy, and commitment to do it?**

The Ecology Of Dream Practices: Finding A Balance

One of the basic requirements for dream practices such as lucidity is getting enough rest and sleep. When you start any dream practices it is important that you really want to do it. You are reading this dream now and you may or may not be compelled to begin these practices. If you decide to commit yourself to it, then it has the potential to interrupt energy that is now being used in other areas of your life. We all have an unlimited amount of energy available to us, although at times our physical body cannot handle these unlimited amounts of energy. **If you are already feeling like your life is running at one hundred-and-five percent, then you will have to scale back on something else to carry out dreamtime practices**. It is also quite possible that you might find you get more energy from not sleeping quite so deeply. A meditative sleep can be quite restful. The most important thing is that if you choose to begin these practices you do so in a way that takes into account and supports all the other important areas of your life.

A Personal Example

There was a time several years ago when we decided we were going to do whatever it takes. We had dabbled with lucid dreaming and had some success, but we were not satisfied with the consistency of our results. We decided we would learn to become lucid and we would do whatever it took. No more casual grazing, we would develop the skills and that was that. We purchased a **Dream Link**™ from Stephen LaBerge's Lucidity

Institute (see Resources section at end of book for details). The Dream Link™ was the first economical aid to lucid dreaming. Previously he had introduced the Dream Light™ which was the instrument that he had developed for use in his lucidity research. They were both based on the ingeniously simple principle of introducing a stimulus (red flashing lights) at precisely the time when a sleeping person would be in REM. The idea was that the light would manifest some way in the dream and it would serve as a dream sign, or a cue, to the conscious mind to wake up in the dream.

The Dream Link™ looks very much like a mask which can aid sleep during the day. You put it over your eyes and secure it with velcro. It contains a timer which you set so that the lights blink when you are in REM. Between the eyes on the front of the mask is a button that serves the same purpose as the reality test which we discussed earlier in the book. To check and see if you are in a dream, you push the button. In ordinary reality when you press the button, it turns the lights off. If you press the button and the lights are turned off, then you know you are really awake. If you think you pressed the button and the lights keep flashing, then you know you are in a dream. LaBerge's research indicates that machines rarely work in dreams in the way they do in the waking state. Therefore when you think you have pressed the button and it does not work, this tells you that you are dreaming. This is a fairly reliable way to verify that a dream is occurring.

We bought our Dream Link™ when we were teaching a Hawaiian Huna Intensive with Tad James and Ardie Flynn. This was a great time to begin using it, since we were teaching spiritual practices, and we also needed to have a good night's sleep. Being the enthusiasts that we are, we decided to try it out on our first night in Hawaii. For the next several nights our sleep was less than restful! It seemed so alien to wear that mask! When I set the timer the first few nights, I was so preoccupied with getting to sleep to make sure that the lights would start flashing while I was in REM, that I kept myself awake! Eventually I fell asleep, only to wake myself up when the lights started flashing. It took a little time to adjust the brightness, frequency, and duration of the lights so that they would register in my dream but not wake me up from physiological sleep. Some mornings I would awaken with the Dream Link™ on the floor, having unconsciously ripped it off in the middle of the night to have some rest! After about four nights of this I was getting a little grumpy: no lucid dreams. No restful sleep. Just this process alone was bringing up all my beliefs about getting a good night's sleep as well as my commitment to the process. Was all of this really worth it?

Around the fifth night I decided to take a break from wearing the mask and something very interesting happened. That night in my dream, I am working on the rear wheel of a bike, but there is a problem. I cannot see the wheel very well; something is obstructing my vision. All of a sudden, I reach up to my face and realize that I have the Dream Link™ on while I am fixing the wheel. I think to myself, "Why do I have this damned thing on?" Like a bolt of lightning my conscious mind pierces the dream and I realize I am in a dream. I am lucid!

To make lucid dreaming easier, there is a more recent product called the **Nova Dreamer™** which detects REM automatically. The timer no longer needs programming so **things can happen automatically.**

This incident illustrates how this path can be. It takes a delicate balance of commitment and enthusiasm, with a bit of detachment. If you want lucidity too much, you do not relax enough to enter the natural cycle of sleep, and this will bring up issues for you to examine. It also teaches you how your unconscious mind works and offers you the possibility of trusting it even more deeply. As soon as I stopped trying so hard, my unconscious mind used the seeds that were planted. It knew what my conscious intention was and it served me. The moral of the story is: take your time. **You will get there, and you might get there just when you least expect it.**

It Is Just A Matter Of Time

One of the standard techniques for lucid dreaming is to wake up *before* you have finished sleeping. Sleep cycles last anywhere from ninety to one hundred-and-twenty minutes. So, to do this, you need to wake up about one hundred minutes before you usually get up—this is just before you begin your last sleep cycle. Stay **awake** for that full cycle and then return to sleep. This optimizes your chances of having a lucid dream. Frequently, within five minutes of going back to sleep, dreaming will begin and will continue for almost the entire cycle. By waking up early, and staying awake for a full cycle, you will be in temporary REM deficit which leads into extended REM once you return to sleep. This same scenario occurs if you get up really early in the morning and then take a nap in the afternoon. In the nap, there is the potential for you to go right into a dream cycle, because of REM deficit from the morning.

The easiest time to go directly from waking into dreaming with little or no sleep, is during the daytime. This was standard practice for Europeans who were lucid dreaming enthusiasts in the 1800s and early 1900s. By napping in the afternoon, they would very quickly enter the dream state. We have used this successfully, particularly on vacation because then we can take a nap! At around four or four-thirty in the afternoon we lie down and the dream theater opens. Becoming lucid at this time of day is easiest if you begin a "mantra" meditation while in the waking state.

A "mantra" is a sacred sound that carries a special resonance which depotentiates conscious processing and transcends the ego. There are numerous mantras that can be found in sacred texts some of which are specifically used for dreaming practices. chapter 7 contains **The Practice Of The Natural Light** which includes a mantra for lucidity. We have used our transcendental meditation mantras, as well as the Hawaiian chant **Moe Uhane** (see Dreamtime Interlude 7) which is taught on the *Huna Intensive* course in Hawaii.

If you do not have a mantra, you can repeat the phrase, "I am awake in a dream," or "Now I am dreaming," or any other variation. If you use a sentence, make sure it is succinct. In one of our other programs, *Mind Power for Life*™, we suggest the mantra, "**I am**." You repeat the mantra as you fall asleep and continue it as you enter the dream state. In this way you have used the mantra as a seed of consciousness that can transcend the usual barrier of sleep. It is like a conscious messenger from the waking state entering the dream state. This method works so well, especially while napping, because there is less slow-wave sleep then. The barrier of sleep is briefer and more transparent than at night, particularly compared to the first two sleep cycles. Normally you would have to be asleep for at least sixty to ninety minutes before beginning your first dream. Attempting lucidity with any technique during the first sleep cycle at night is challenging.

Another aid to lucid dreaming that we have never seen documented elsewhere is jet lag. We are reminded of this right now because we are writing this section in an airport! Associations are wonderful things! Jet lag is useful for something! It is very easy to access that dreamy state if you are recovering from an eastbound trip with a significant time change. Again, it becomes a matter of timing and ecology. Make sure that your conscious and unconscious minds are aligned about carrying out dreaming practices at this time. Also, make sure that you do not have anything too pressing that might create time conflicts.

Knowing What Or Who To Look For

We began our lucid dreaming efforts after reading Carlos Castaneda's work. The instructions that he was given by his teacher, don Juan Matus, are well known in dreamwork circles. He asked Carlos to look for his hands while dreaming and to focus on them. Even though some people have told us that they learned lucid dreaming this way, our results were less than gratifying! However, the underlying structure of don Juan's instructions is important. It is necessary to establish a link between our waking lives and our dreaming lives; first, by making distinctions between the two, and then, by learning to recognize natural points of intersection. In our system, this would be equivalent to **using**

incubation to establish a cue for lucidity. Decide on a specific object that will serve as a cue. Then use the incubation process in chapter 4 and go to sleep.

A variation of this idea is to incubate an entire dream context. Rather than picking an object such as your hands, you could incubate a geographic location. This was another technique used in don Juan's teachings. He would ask Carlos to go to a "power spot" that he had visited in his waking reality, and make that the backdrop for his dreamscape. An advantage to this approach is that it automatically activates in the dream the resource states associated with the power spot. It is a way of creating a context of resourcefulness that is transferred from the waking state to the dream state. It also creates **a bridge from the waking state through the sleep state into the dream state**.

Do you have a favorite place? Maybe it is a vacation spot, or a place you always wanted to visit, and, once you finally did, it was everything you desired. How about a place where you had to perform in some way and you did superbly? We carry out a lot of training in our office, so one of our power spots is our office. The key is to pick a spot that has a lot of "positive" emotion attached to it. A good indication of this is how you feel when you first think about the spot. If you have a strong sweep of emotion when you think about it, that is good. If you have a fast automatic response, then you know it is wired to lots of positive associations at the unconscious level.

Another similar idea is to follow this same process with a person for whom you have strong positive feelings. You will have better results if you actually discuss this with the person. It will reinforce your intention for your unconscious mind. **An advanced dreaming technique is for both people to incubate a meeting with each other in their dreams**. This can be done lucidly or non-lucidly. Even in the case of a non-lucid dream, this can be exciting and can deepen your relationship with one another. There are a couple of intriguing possibilities here. First, let's say that you plan to dream about the other. The next day you check with each other and compare notes. Did you actually experience the person in the same image as in the waking state? If so, were you both dreaming the same content? Most of the time this might not happen, but it is possible and is certainly evidence of a deep connection with your own unconscious and higher conscious mind, as well as with your dream partner. If you were not dreaming the same content, still compare the dreams. If you would like to, interpret them in the way we described in chapter 5. What meaning do they have for each of you when considered together?

Another possible scenario is that you both did the incubation and you did not see the other person in your dreams. This happens quite frequently, but it does not mean that you were not in each others' dreams. Maybe you **felt** the other's presence. It is quite possible that your unconscious mind may symbolize the person in some other way, so you still **feel** the way you do when you are near them. However, in the dream you did not experience them in the same physical image as in waking reality.

By now, you might be starting to consider what it would be like to arrange a meeting with another person on the dream plane, become lucid, and begin to develop a conscious dream relationship. One of our friends belonged to a group who met regularly in their dreams at a university of "higher" learning on the astral plane. A word of caution here. Including others in your dreams requires the same responsibilities and consequences as including them in your waking life. We strongly suggest that you fully consider your motives and intentions before pursuing this path. As far as we can tell, the Law of Karma is a part of all the realities we have explored!

The Royal Road To Lucidity: Dream Signs

Another effective means to bridging consensual waking reality and dream reality is by what Stephen LaBerge refers to as "dream signs" (LaBerge & Rheingold, 1990). **Dream signs are those occurrences in dreams that could not** (at least under most normal circumstances) **happen in our waking state**. For example, if I consistently find animals talking in my dreams, this is a reliable dream sign, and I can use it to help me become lucid. In most cases our dreams are loaded with phenomena that are very unlikely in the consensual waking state. We are so easily swept up in our own story lines or delusions that we do not recognize them as such when we are dreaming. When we are in the midst of a dream, it is as real as real can be. We do not usually question its veracity. We just go along with the flow. Therefore learning to become lucid, as we mentioned earlier in the book, requires commitment, clarity of intention, and energy.

There are two primary ways to identify and utilize dream signs. The first relies on a dream journal. Collect approximately two weeks' worth of dream entries and look over them, sorting for common objects, occurrences, people, and dreamscapes. Highlight those that are repetitive. These are the natural dream signs that your unconscious mind likes to use.

The second way combines using your dream signs with **The Dreaming Meditation Technique** (see Dreamtime Interlude 6). Several times a day, or whenever you use the dream meditation, at the deepest phase of your meditation imagine experiencing the dream sign as if you were in a dream. Then do the reality test covered in Dreamtime Interlude 1 as if you are doing it in a dream. Ask yourself, "**Is this a dream?**" and answer as if it is a dream, since you will be in the same state as when you are dreaming. This is a powerful way to build a bridge from waking to dreaming.

Tranceporting Yourself To Lucidity

Another approach which worked well for us was using hypnosis as a vehicle to incubate and rehearse lucid dreaming. Since the states of trance and REM are so similar, it seemed to be an easy way to build a bridge between them. Our ideas are supported by the research on state-dependent learning, which says that whatever you learn in a particular state will be best recalled in that same state. So why not build in all the resources necessary to access lucid dreaming inside hypnosis? We can then make suggestions to the unconscious mind about its ability to help us become lucid and ask for its cooperation to do so. Knowing how to induce trance in yourself or others is a viable way to propagate lucid dreams. If you do not know how to induce trance, that is okay because **The Dreaming Meditation Technique** (see Dreamtime Interlude 6) will do it for you.

If you are interested in generating hypnotic dreams to rehearse skills transferable to dreams unconsciously and consciously, we suggest you read chapter 10 of our earlier book, *Training Trances*. **Alternatively, you can continue reading over the unconscious reviews. Each one of these was, in part, written to help stimulate the processes involved in lucid dreaming**. While hypnosis seems an obvious choice to stimulate lucid dreaming, there is very little written about it in the lucid dreaming literature. LaBerge, who is the most pre-eminent lucid dream researcher in the United States, began to embrace hypnosis for enhancing lucid dreaming only in his second book (LaBerge & Rheingold, 1990) and then more fully in his later work (1991). He mentions it briefly in his first book, *Lucid Dreaming*, and he now also has a tape available which provides hypnotic suggestions for lucid dreaming.

If you decide to use a hypnosis tape to induce lucid dreaming, we have found it best to use the tape during the day, well before going to sleep. Incubation before going to bed is fine because it only takes a few minutes. I learned this lesson the hard way when I really became very interested in lucid dreaming a few years ago and decided to make a hypnosis tape to use every night before going to bed. I was really excited about its accelerating my lucid dreaming practices.

I listened to the tape for several nights just before falling asleep. It was the first time in my entire life that I did not remember a single dream! It not only had the effect of preventing me from dreaming lucidly, it also totally blocked everything that was happening from the time I went to sleep until I woke up. I was putting too much energy into it at one time rather than allowing my body or unconscious mind to relax into it. It was very much like our Dream Link™ experiences—remember the delicate balance between intention and detachment? So I stopped listening to the tape for a couple of days. I then started listening to it during the day for a few days and finally I stopped listening to it altogether. Seven days later, I had two lucid dreams! One of these dreams was one of the most memorable and transcendental experiences I have ever had. Here is what I recorded in my dream journal.

A Dream

I am walking on a hill of devastation. There are dirt and bodies. I am alone and feeling hopelessness and despair. I see a man with a gun and tell him I do not care what he does. We have a disagreement, but I do not know what it is. We fight and I take away the gun and win the fight. I look up toward the horizon, across a body of neon-blue water and see a city made of Greek-looking temples like the Parthenon and behind them is a fiery sunset, more vivid than I have ever seen. I am in awe and say out loud, "This is so beautiful." I have never seen colors so vibrant. They are shiny and that makes them look absolutely surreal. The beauty and surrealism of the colors make me realize I am in a dream. I feel total exhilaration sweep over me.

I am conscious. This feeling soon threatens my ability to stay in the dream. I feel myself beginning to slip toward waking consciousness. I remember that LaBerge suggests "spinning" to stay lucid (*Lucid Dreaming*, 1986). So I begin to spin myself (the consciousness of who I am in this dream) around and around until I really feel myself spinning upward. It works—I am still lucid.

I take off and begin to fly, still spinning. I spin myself into the dark, purple black of space. I am completely aware. I am in the Void, or as the Hawaiians call it, the I'o, the source of everything, the unmanifest. It is so peaceful and quiet, although I am experiencing the sound of space. I am still spinning, feeling exhilaration, and in wonder of what is happening. I look around and can see what I intuitively know are thoughtforms floating through space. I do not know how I know, I just know. They seem to be the configurations of light, branch-like, and not unlike some Hawaiian symbols I have studied. I just stay in this state and eventually wake up.

A few days later, I had a second dream about the I'o. I asked my unconscious mind to incubate a dream where I would transcend something material that in the waking state would not be possible for me. I am in a kitchen, trying to start a microwave oven; I keep pushing the button and it does not turn on. I keep pressing it, thinking, "What is wrong with this anyway?" At that moment I realize I am in a dream and become lucid. Once again the excitement catapults me toward the waking state, but at that moment I start to spin. I lift off, transcending the kitchen ceiling and the roof of the house. Then I go all the way up into the I'o.

Incubating Lucidity

The next method we recommend for achieving lucidity is a hybrid of an approach codified by Stephen LaBerge called the **Mnemonic Induction of Lucid Dreams**—MILD (*Lucid Dreaming*, 1986). We should note that this technique can also be used therapeutically to complete or resolve non-lucid dreams as well. **The basis of this technique is to establish the intention of waking up after each dream period**. You set the intention before going to sleep. Each time you awaken, recall as many details as possible from the dreams. Now set your intention to remember that you are dreaming and then imagine you have gone back into the dream. See yourself in the dream and recognize that it is a dream. Imagine finding dream signs and saying to yourself, "I am dreaming." Repeat the intention and the dream rehearsal several times and then fall asleep. This technique is effective and easy to do. Through our experiences we have modified LaBerge's MILD technique. It builds upon what we have already covered up to this point.

In the incubation phase, we suggest that you use the dream incubation technique to set your intention. The advantage of this is that you are entering an altered state that is basically the same as the dream state. This means that you will have state-specific learning working for you. You will be setting the intention from inside the dream state in advance, which makes it more likely that you will remember that you are dreaming and/or you will remember to wake up after the dream period.

Often this preparation together with all the other techniques we have discussed so far, particularly the reality testing and the dreaming meditation, will be more than enough to consistently produce lucid dreams. It is important that you use these procedures regularly. Remember: it will be easier if you set your intention for dream periods closer to dawn because then you will be dreaming for longer periods of time.

If you do not become lucid and wake up after the dream period, then do as LaBerge suggests in *Lucid Dreaming*: remember as many details from the dream as possible. Then, once again, carry out a brief incubation and imagine going right back into the dream you just had as if it were continuing. This, by the way, is also an excellent way to complete nonlucid dreams for therapeutic purposes. In this case, you imagine the dream resolving or ending exactly the way you want.

The key to going back into the same dream is to notice whether you were associated or dissociated from your body in the dream. Associated means that you will see what you see, hear what you hear, feel what you feel, as if it is happening now. Dissociated means that you are outside the space of your body. If you have good recall, it is beneficial to remember the point of view or angle that your body was in. This is somewhat different from LaBerge's instructions to see yourself in the dream.

Next, complete the rehearsal by imagining that you notice a dream sign and ask yourself, "Is this a dream?" or "Am I dreaming?". We recommend that you **say the exact phrase** that you have used during the day for reality testing (see Dreamtime Interlude 1). The more you repeat this during the day, the more likely it is to seep into your dreams. By using the same words you benefit from the conditioning of the reality test in the waking state.

If you do not find it easy to fall back to sleep, that is okay; just repeat the rehearsal until you feel drowsy enough to sleep. If you sleep very deeply, we suggest that you sit up in bed to carry out the rehearsal so your intention is strong enough to register with your unconscious mind.

The Technique

1. **Use the Dream Incubation procedure** (see chapter 4) before going to bed to set your intention to become lucid in the dream and/or wake up at the end of the dream period. (Closer to dawn is best.)

2. **Recall as much of the dream as possible.** Note any dream signs and whether you are associated or dissociated.

3. **Use the Dream Incubation procedure to rehearse going back in the dream.**

4. **Notice a dream sign and carry out the reality test** while you are completing the rehearsal. (For therapeutic completion of non-lucid dreams, imagine the outcome the way you want it. You can, of course, also complete the dream lucidly to create a therapeutic resolution.)

A Completion Dream Turned Lucid: Knowing Just Enough To Face The Demon

This is a dream that I had late January 1996, while in Acapulco. Julie was taking a PhotoReading™ Instructors' Training there. After initially deciding not to go, I re-decided and joined her. We had not seen each other for a little over a week, so I was in a grateful mood for being with her in such a beautiful part of the world. I had missed her. The weather at home was dismal.

The hours of Julie's training were quite long, unpredictable, and the training itself was a logistics nightmare. Not being a part of training, yet being around it, was a strange circumstance for me. I am used to being quite involved because I co-teach many trainings! I had a lot of time to myself. I was in one of those periods when I was feeling a lot and feeling it deeply. I was planning to complete a number of work-related projects while she was in class. After a day or two of taking it easy, I decided to begin work again on this dream book. It had been an on-again-off-again project for us. Each time I would think about starting, I would find something else to do. I was feeling really stuck. That night I had a dream.

The Dream

Julie and I are in a doctor's office. A nurse whom I do not trust is there. In fact, the whole situation seems wrong. The nurse is explaining something to Julie about taking a test. Somehow I realize that Julie is not just getting a simple test but that she is getting a whole battery of tests (for something serious, I fear). I look at Julie and she tries to smile at me, but her upper lip quivers, like she wants to cry, though she is stifling it. At that point I start getting angry at the nurse and start saying something like, "This is a f*****g mess; what the hell do you think you are doing—and I am not apologizing for saying f**k either, because I am angry." With that, I follow the nurse into another room, still arguing with her. She is not really reacting strongly in any way. She pulls out what looks like a large bundle of gauze packing. I presume it is going to be used for some procedure that she is going to run on Julie. I ask her what it is for. She replies, "I am going to soak this in pills." I feel a rush of fear, and, for a fleeting moment, I notice in the periphery a young man, in his twenties with dark hair, standing in the doorway. In a split second, before I awaken, I recognize him from the previous dream I had earlier in the night. He was with some people who were in some way against me, causing some kind of trouble.

I wake up and stay motionless. I am lying on my left side with my arms somewhat folded. I keep my eyes closed and decide that I do not like the dream. I am upset with myself for waking up so early in the dream even though it was not all that scary. I decide that the man is the "problem", the symbol for something I have to face. I decide how I want the dream to end. "Julie and I are safe and healthy and we go on living happily," I think to myself, while in a half-asleep, half-awake state. It is hard to keep my train of thought going. It takes so much effort, my mind wants to slip away in some other direction, but I keep bringing it back to finish the dream. After a few moments I see the man appear in my visual field. I am not sure if I am in a dream or lucid or if I am awake. Confusing. I feel like he is the Devil. I grab a cross and move toward him and try to push the cross into his chest. He does not want this but is not really fighting back. It just seems as though he is backing up as I push the cross into his chest. I start saying: "Be one with God. Be one with God. Be one with God." As I keep saying this over and over again, I become lucid and continue chanting this and the figure dissolves, while I think that it is some energy that needs to leave me. At that point I actually wake up and my whole body has goose-flesh that keeps coming in waves for several minutes. It really feels like something is leaving me.

I wrote in my journal, "I am not entirely sure what this was about, but I did need to finish the dream and feel complete about it." That morning I woke up feeling totally renewed and inspired. I recounted the dream to Julie and she was even more excited by it. During the subsequent weeks, I felt as creative and free as I ever felt. The writing just flowed. Sometimes in dreams, like the rest of life, you do not have to know the details. I only knew what I needed to know to go back into the dream and resolve it. Even now this dream is a mystery to me and, in this case, I like it that way.

Using Pendulum Techniques To Create Lucidity

If you like working with a pendulum and it produces consistent results for you, here is another variation to incubate lucidity. Use the unconscious review technique from the **Getting To Know Your Higher Conscious Mind Interlude** (see Dreamtime Interlude 5). This will enable you to activate all the relevant resources and abilities to dream lucidly. This technique can work whether or not you have ever had a lucid dream. First of all, it is quite likely that you had spontaneous lucid dreams at earlier points in your life and do not remember them. It is not unusual for younger children to dream lucidly, but never recognize they are lucid.

Additionally, remember that prior to the age of four most of us do not discriminate as yet between dreaming and waking reality, let alone lucidity and non-lucidity. One could suggest that lucid dreams were never labelled as "lucid," or actually were mislabelled. In such cases, using the unconscious review will give the unconscious mind the freedom to review any memories or dreams that, when activated, could produce reference experiences for our present purposes.

In the rare case that your unconscious mind may have no intact memories of dreaming lucidly, that is fine. It can **construct** the resources necessary to dream lucidly **now** by bringing together the appropriate experiences for developing the skill.

An additional action with the pendulum is to ask for permission from the unconscious mind to support the conscious mind to dream lucidly. Then have the unconscious mind identify a time in the future **after** which it has had a lucid dream. This is a standard hypnotic technique (used for therapeutic issues) which also works well to install future abilities.

The Technique

1. **Establish "yes," "no," and "not ready to consciously know, yet" signals from the pendulum.**

2. **Get permission from and align the unconscious and conscious minds**. Ask, *"Are you, the unconscious mind, willing to support my lucid dreaming practices?"* If you get a "no" response, ask what is preventing its support and use the **Unconscious Interview and Clearing Technique** (see Dreamtime Interlude 4). In fact, whenever you get a "no" response, use the clearing technique.

3. **Ask the unconscious mind if it will move to a time in the future when you will have had a lucid dream**. (You could also ask it to move further out to a point where you have been dreaming lucidly for a consistent period.) Ask, *"Will you, the unconscious mind, move to a point sometime in the future where I have had a lucid dream?"* or *"Will you, the unconscious mind, move forward to a point at some time in the future when I have been dreaming lucidly for a consistent period?"*

4. **Direct the unconscious mind to identify the time when you are dreaming lucidly**. Say, *"Please go to that point in the future where I have been lucidly dreaming (consistently) and signal with a 'yes' response once you have located it."*

5. **Direct the unconscious mind to review the future memory.** Say, *"Please review this future event outside my conscious awareness until you have completely integrated the experience now, and signal with a 'yes' when you begin the review."* Then, after you receive a "yes," say, *"Please signal with a 'no' response when you no longer have to review the memory because it is integrated."*

6. **Ask for permission for conscious appreciation of the future memory.** Ask, *"Is it okay for me to know consciously about the memory?"*"If you get a "yes" response direct it to let you review it consciously. If you get a "no," that is okay, thank your unconscious mind for helping you and look forward to being pleasantly surprised at some time in the future! The key here is to cooperate with your unconscious. Remember everything is designed to produce alignment.

Although these techniques are not foolproof, **they will greatly increase your chances of having lucid dreams in a short amount of time**. Use all of the tools at your disposal until you find those that work best for you. It is important to continue with the reality testing and dreaming meditation, particularly if you are going to progress to more advanced levels of dreaming practices.

Conscious Review Of Chapter 6

1. **Lucid dreaming is the ability to be consciously aware of dreaming while in a dream**—to transcend the consensual reality in which we live, the "real" one.

2. **Lucid dreaming models the principle of creation**. When we are dreaming lucidly, we are as close as most of us will ever be to an experience of total, raw creation.

3. **Once lucidity occurs, there are lots of choices—anything is possible**. The usual constraints are lifted. We now have conscious choice to create and design our reality.

4. **To begin lucid dreaming practices you want to recall at least two dreams per night**. If you do, then you have enough rapport with your unconscious mind to begin lucid dreaming practices. Otherwise, increasing your recall (see below) is the first and most important step.

5. **There are two easy ways to structure your intention to dream lucidly**. The first is to keep a dream journal and the second is to incubate recall, using the method outlined in chapter 4.

6. **The easiest time to go directly from waking into dreaming with little or no sleep is during the daytime**. Becoming lucid at this time of day is easiest if you begin a mantra meditation while in the waking state.

7. **Dream signs are those occurrences in dreams that could not happen in our waking state**.

8. **There are two primary ways to identify and utilize dream signs.** The first is to collect two weeks' worth of dream entries in your journal. Sort through them noticing common objects, occurrences, people, and dreamscapes. The second is to use the Dreaming Meditation Technique (Dreamtime Interlude 6). Several times a day, or at the deepest phase of your meditation, imagine experiencing the dream sign as if you are in a dream; carry out the reality test, answering as if you are dreaming.

9. **Hypnosis, dream incubation, LaBerge's MILD technique, and the pendulum may be used to create lucidity**. Use all of the tools at your disposal until you find what works best for you. Keep the reality testing and dreaming meditation going, particularly if you are going to progress to more advanced levels of dreaming practices.

Unconscious Review Of Chapter 6

As you know by now, we all dream. Some people dream during the day. Some dream during the night. Some people spend time dreaming when they are awake and others are awake when they dream. Whether or not you ***remember your dreams*** or just ***remember you are dreaming in a dream*** is not as important as remembering dreams can have lasting, profound, beneficial effects that can stay with you for the rest of your life. We do not know when you will find yourself getting very ***curious*** about your ability to dream lucidly; to ***become consciously aware*** that you are dreaming ***when you are in a dream***. Perhaps tonight, perhaps it will take a few days for your ***motivation and curiosity to build*** before you begin to set your intention to ***wake up in a dream***. At this point we have ***know way*** of knowing when your unconscious and higher conscious minds will make the decision to let you experience the conscious act of creation that occurs each night as you dream. We only know that the mere fact that you have read this book this far and are reading this now means ***you are aligning your intention*** at a deeper level than you could ever know consciously. We also know that reading about lucid dreaming...and thinking about it often during the day...very often results in having a ***spontaneous*** lucid dream.

Perhaps you may find yourself searching for dream signs in your dreams or maybe you will prefer reality testing and asking, by the way, "Is this a dream?...Am I dreaming?" We do not know. We only know that all scientific evidence suggests that ***intention*** is the greatest factor in ***remembering*** to ***wake up in a dream*** when you are dreaming. How you ***set your intention*** is totally up to you. Whether you do it as we have explained is not as important as really affirming to your unconscious mind that ***you are ready*** to ***have a lucid dream***...remember...you have the opportunity every night of your life, several times each night. Maybe your unconscious mind will surprise you and you will have a lucid dream when you least expect, or maybe it will be a gradual process of false awakenings until you finally ***remember to ask*** in a dream "***Is this a dream?***...Is this a dream?...Is this a dream?...Is this a dream?...Is this a dream?"...And ***realize***....to your surprise that ***you are awake and in a dream.***

Chapter 7

Beyond Lucidity:
Finding The "I" In Light

Throughout this book, we have outlined a dream system whose purpose is to create alignment among the conscious, unconscious, and higher conscious minds. We have said that no matter which path you choose in this dream system, you will ultimately foster this alignment. You can do so through the dream meditation and reality testing, through incubation, through interpretation, and through lucid dreaming. What we have never asked explicitly was, **"For what higher purpose would we want to become proficient at any one of these techniques or, for that matter, achieve alignment among the three minds?"**

As we develop dreaming practices and explore the seemingly unlimited realm of dreams, we will probably engage in what some call "ego fulfillment." This is where we choose to do things that cater for unmet desires in our waking state. We have certainly done this. At first there is the novelty of dreaming lucidly, which is, believe us, awesome! The first couple of times we became lucid, we were so excited that we woke ourselves up right away, feeling, "**OH MY, I AM LUCID**!......Oh, this is great," and then we would be awake and it would be over. We would literally wake ourselves up from the lucid dream because of our own excitement. We remember similar experiences when we were first experimenting with peripheral vision and other meditation techniques. We would get to a place where everything was quiet, with no internal dialogue and all of sudden, "Yippie, my internal dialogue stopped...how awesome...ooops!" Balance!

After learning to dream lucidly, you might incubate and have lucid dreams strictly for pleasure. You might have a romantic evening with Sharon Stone, play guitar with the Beatles, or play basketball with Michael Jordan. The list can go on forever. We have known people who have incubated some really outrageous dreams. Balance!

As far as we can tell this is a learning process, and not one worth interrupting just because it would be more "spiritual" to be meditating in a lucid dream instead. **At the same time, who or what you create in your dreams is parallel to, and reflective of, your evolution as a human being and as a spirit**. It is all a matter of balance and learning. As far as we can tell there are no short-cuts—and there is really no reason for any anyway! We are all on the path to Enlightenment and we will all get there when we do. In the classic yoga text, *Autobiography Of A Yogi* (1946, p.120), Yogananda says that we are all headed for enlightenment and that, according to Hindu scriptures, it will take about a million years of incarnating to reach it.

As we see it, we chose to come into this life to learn; to learn what it is to experience Spirit, God, and the Universe through the limitations and possibilities of the physical plane. The fruit is here for the picking. While it can bring us pleasure, it is a clear example of the relativity and impermanence of a physical world. Our ego and its demands also illustrate the relativity and impermanence of this life. **Dreaming practices are no more of a guarantee to fast enlightenment than any other spiritual system**. Dreams serve as mirrors that reflect the light that is exposed to them; we can either look at, deny, or look through these mirrors. We have free choice. It is all a process; a process, some would say, of finding our way back to the Light.

The Practice Of Natural Light

When the state of dreaming has dawned,
Do not lie in ignorance like a corpse.
Enter the natural sphere of unwavering attentiveness.
Recognize your dreams and transform illusion into luminosity.
Do not sleep like an animal.
Do the practice which mixes sleep and reality.

From *Dream Yoga And The Practice of Natural Light*
by Namkhai Norbu

One Buddhist master compared lucid dreaming, simply for the sake of lucid dreaming, to games: it is nothing more than ego fulfillment that keeps the illusion of separateness alive (Norbu & Katz, 1992). He was obviously either advanced on the path or quite repressed! Seriously, though, in the **Dzogchen Night Practice of the White Light** or in **Tantric Dream Yoga**, lucidity is but a phase or, in some cases, a by-product of one's spiritual development. The emphasis is on presence and awareness, rather than the ability to dream lucidly. In the Dzogchen school the primary utility of lucidity is to become one with the light. It teaches us how to transcend our sleep and later our death.

What happens every night when we fall asleep? We lose our senses, the mechanisms that in many cases let us know that we are alive. We fall into a period of unconsciousness that we referred to earlier as non-REM sleep. It is the time when we are so deeply asleep that we are, as the expression goes, "dead to the world." We move from being awake, to losing awareness of our senses, to losing touch with reality as we usually know it, to going through this dark tunnel of deep sleep. At night as we sleep, the "light" at the other end of the tunnel is our dream state. Intense mental activity begins again—every bit as intense as in our waking state, but a separate reality. We have sensory experience, but it is all internally generated and done with little, if any, reflexive consciousness—unless, of course, we have developed lucidity. Then what happens? We go back into deep slumber (non-REM) and continue this four or five times each night until we wake up in the morning. **Is there a metaphor here for life and death**? Dzogchen Practitioners of the Natural Light believe so, and so do we.

What happens when we die? First, all senses begin to withdraw and eventually they vanish. We become unconscious. Eventually, according to Dream Yoga scriptures, our consciousness slowly returns. This is the passage of the Natural Light. The question is, "Will we be conscious enough to see it and make a conscious choice to join it or not?"

The Bardos

In Dzogchen sect of Tibetan Buddhism there are "in between" or intermediate states of consciousness called **Bardos**. There are six Bardos. The first is our **ordinary waking state**. It is our consensual reality. The one we learned was the "real" reality. The second is the **dream state** that we experience while we are in physiological sleep. It is the state that points to possibilities existing beyond the realm of our waking, consensual reality. The third includes **meditative and trance states**. Mastering access to the third Bardo enables us to bridge the first two Bardo states. We have spent a fair amount of time discussing hypnosis, meditation, and incubation because they themselves are a Bardo. They can be used to link the first two, as well as prepare for the transcendence of the next three Bardos.

The fourth Bardo is the **process of dying** where the elements comprising our body dissolve. Mastering the first three Bardos prepares us for our physical dissolution. **Lucid dreaming in this lifetime makes it possible to transcend the dream of death, the fourth Bardo**. Each night as we sleep we have the opportunity to wake up and be conscious through each intermediate state. In this way, we have choice.

The fifth Bardo is the **Bardo of reality**. In this state we have the opportunity to recognize that we mistake our representations for true reality. Dreaming practices are a fundamental way of transcending this illusion. This is really the reason why we wrote this book, and the purpose of the spiritual system we are proposing. As we learn more about our dreams we can begin to accept more responsibility for their contents. Incubation and lucidity provide us with the ability to confront and transform the images which we may encounter in our dreams. It helps us remember who creates the dreams in the first place.

Everything we encounter in our dreams is of our own making and arises from our thoughts. Our thoughts are observations which we use to create something from the unmanifest manifest—the Void, nothingness. Experiences of the fifth Bardo take us back to the source, the point, from a quantum physics view, where creation begins. Here the probability wave becomes a particle. Here the illusions based upon the relativity of our sensory perception are born. One of those illusions is the illusion of "I" as a separate ego.

The sixth Bardo is the **search for rebirth**. It is the choice of our next incarnation. It is where we can find the Light if we are awake. It is the ultimate choice: to rejoin the Source and to recognize **ALL THAT IS**. We can actually be totally conscious of every life that we have lived and will live as we make our transition. We have a choice of going into the light, or not, at this point. Here we have totally free choice to be reincarnated or not. In some circumstances we may be asked to enter physical form, even though we are beyond having to learn things to become enlightened. These people are known as "**avatars**," people who are born as fully realized individuals, like Sai Baba in India or Mother Meera in Germany. They are here to carry out a higher purpose or global mission for mankind.

One of the striking features of the Tibetan description of the Bardos is that they are all just "intermediate states" (Norbu & Katz, 1992). They are only part of the picture. This idea is really worth contemplating and meditating on: none of these states is the whole picture, but we seduce ourselves into thinking it is. Many of us go through our entire life thinking that our waking state is the whole picture. Often we make the same mistake when we dream. In our introduction we talk about how real dreams seem to be while we are in them. We have been conditioned to think that dreams are less important when we are awake. Yet, while we dream, that is all there is. The same is true about our perception of reality, and of life and of death.

The Hawaiian Perspective

In Hawaiian culture, it is said that a thin veil separates the spirit world from the physical, the living from the dead, the wave from the particle. Their perception of time is compatible with that of the Dzogchen Buddhists and the quantum physicists. **They believe that the past, present, and future, as we know them, all occur simultaneously on different frequencies**, just as in the sixth Bardo when one passes over and is awake, all lifetimes are available as reflections of the one, the Light.

Before native Hawaiians die, they often have full knowledge of their impending death. They usually die late in life, at a time when they are ready. Many receive a sign about their death through a dream, usually a night or two before they die. A messenger, a symbol from the higher conscious mind, comes to them in their dream and tells them to prepare. Then, traditionally, they will gather their family together, letting them know that the time has come, and prepare them for the future. If they have special spiritual powers, they will pass their "mana," or life force energy, to the next person who will take over for them. **Then they prepare themselves, lie down, and quietly, with full awareness, pass over into the next reality**.

The Practice Of The Night

In many ways the Practice of the Night is the simplest of all the practices in this book. Simplest, but not necessarily the easiest. It is very similar to the technique mentioned in the previous chapter where you use a mantra to move directly from waking to dreaming. We suggested there that the easiest time to use this sort of approach is in the afternoon, because we do not usually pass through protracted periods of non-REM sleep in the afternoon. **In the Practice of the Night, as you lie down to sleep, you meditate on a symbol or mantra, and continue to do so throughout the entire night**. That is it. In the Dzogchen school it is not necessary to remember one's dreams, to interpret them, or even to set lucidity as a goal. The primary focus is awareness, presence, and mindfulness. The perspective of this school is that if you are able to maintain focus on a mantra or visualization, you will naturally develop lucidity over time, as you gain awareness.

We have experimented with this technique and have found it to be worthwhile and challenging. If you want to use the classic way, visualize the letter **"A" in white in the heart chakra**. You should vibrate the sound "Ahhh" in conjunction with the visualization. Depending upon how deeply involved you become with the Dzogchen system, you can visualize the "A" in different colors in the throat or crown chakras for specific purposes. We use our Transcendental Meditation mantras, as well as the Hawaiian Dreamtime chant (see Dreamtime Interlude 7) and various

Hawaiian symbols. For the purposes of our system, you need to have a symbol or mantra that is sufficiently compelling and compatible with the unconscious mind to cause an ecological alteration of awareness. We do not suggest using symbols that you do not know, do not have permission to use, have not been initiated to, or do not "feel" right about when meditating on them.

Another technique involves **holding a stone or crystal** in your hand throughout the night, so you awaken with the stone in your hand. If you have been doing the Dreaming Meditation, this is already set up for you. The stone will serve as an anchor for the dreaming state. It provides a focal point of attention, similar to a kinesthetic mantra. Obviously you can use the stone together with a mantra or visualization, if you wish.

Holding the stone, or repeating a mantra, teaches the delicate balance of intention and non-attachment. It takes practice. If you try too hard, you may keep yourself awake. If you let go completely, you will fall asleep. If you notice dramatic alterations in your sleep activity, we suggest that you stop the practice until you can contact someone who is qualified and knowledgeable in this area. Mild alterations are to be expected. You may notice that your dreams change or your sleep becomes lighter. If this happens, our studies and experience show that this is usually a good sign. Over time, as you carry out the Practice of the Night, your sleep will get lighter *and yet* more restful. One of the beliefs that we all eventually confront as we move down the dream path is what constitutes a good night's sleep. We will give you a clue: it might not be what you were taught to think!

As in the case of basic dreaming practices, what you do during the day has an impact on what happens at night. If you are living a harried life and are exhausting yourself during the day, it is unlikely that you will have the energy and intention to carry out this practice. So take your time. Be patient. Have fun. Enjoy the path and the scenery along the way. The Practice of the Night is a lifelong ritual that will grow as you grow. **Lucidity will happen in time as a natural consequence** and so will much more than you can comprehend!

A Spiritual Initiation

This is the single most powerful dream I have ever had and probably ever will have. For many years I have wanted to visit Sai Baba in India. We almost went there one year but the arrangements did not work out. When we were planning this trip, I received information from Sai Baba's ashram about him. Many believe that he is a fully realized Master, an avatar, who is a living incarnation of God. He performs miracles, many of which have been documented on videotape. Among his materials was a page of information and one line which said, "You have said 'yes' to me." This was a very powerful statement and I took it to mean that by receiving this information I had made a commitment to him. Since I believe he is a living incarnation of God, I was okay with this.

A few months later we were in New Zealand and I was carrying out the Practice of the Night. As I fell asleep I was meditating on an image of Sai Baba. Earlier in the evening I had read a book about Sai Baba, which is a good incubation practice. This book contained a story about a man who had a personal interview with Sai Baba in India. During the interview, Sai Baba asked the man why he had not realized that he (Sai Baba) had come to him in three of his dreams. The man was taken aback and said he never realized it was Sai Baba. I was very impressed with the idea that Sai Baba would take the time to come to us in our dreams—especially if he had never met us before! This was my dream:

The Dream

I am standing outside, looking north, and behind me is a group of people. From in front of me a very large, looming figure comes very quickly toward me. While watching the figure, I begin to back up in the direction of the people. I never reach them. In a split second the figure lunges toward me, falling on me, and absorbs me into his body. At that exact moment, **I have full conscious awareness that it is Sai Baba**. He has come to me, initiated me, and made me one with him. I did not need to go to India to receive his blessings or to become one with him. He has crossed the time-space continuum to make me one with the Divine.

This Book, This Dream

So, throughout this book you may have asked yourself about the purpose of dreaming practices. Are they really designed to develop trust in the unconscious mind? To learn how to incubate dreams for problem solving, creativity, or healing? To interpret dreams as guidance from the higher conscious mind? To dream lucidly to experience the creation of something from nothing? To align the conscious, unconscious, and higher conscious minds? To transcend sleep? To transcend death? To transcend illusion? To be one with the Light from which we all have come? The answer is a resounding "Yes" to all of these, and there is more, much more!

All of these questions can occupy your conscious mind, while a deeper part of you fully considers the main purpose *we* had for writing this book, this dream. **"Has it helped you to discover more fully who you *really* are?"** If your answer to this is "Yes"—to any degree—then we will feel that our purpose in dreaming this dream has been served. We know how much more connected we feel with people, events, and the environment around us from working with our dreams. We have had many powerful, exciting experiences in dreams which have demonstrated our interconnectedness and our ability to transcend the time/space continuum. We have been blessed by our dreams. Our faith in a higher order has increased dramatically by the insights and connections made on the dream plane. So we certainly hope you have enjoyed this dream cycle of ours and that you experience many profound and beneficial effects from your dreams that can stay with *you* for the rest of your life!

Conscious Review Of Chapter 7

1. **The purpose of the dream system introduced in this book is to create alignment among the conscious, unconscious, and higher conscious minds**. No matter which path you choose in this dream system, you will ultimately foster this alignment.

2. **Who or what you create in your dreams is parallel to and reflective of your evolution as a human being and as a spirit.** Dreaming practices are no more of a guarantee to fast enlightenment than any other spiritual system. Dreams serve as mirrors that reflect the light that is exposed to them; we can either look at, deny, or look through these mirrors.

3. **Lucidity is but a phase or, in some cases, a by-product of one's spiritual development in the Night Practice of the White Light and Tantric Dream Yoga.** These paths emphasize presence and awareness, rather than the ability to dream lucidly, which is for the purpose of becoming one with the Light.

4. **Waking, sleeping, and dreaming are metaphors for life and death.**

5. **In certain Buddhist schools, there are Bardos—six "in-between" or intermediate states of consciousness.** Lucid dreaming in this lifetime makes it possible to transcend the dream of death, the fourth Bardo.

6. **In Hawaiian spirituality many believe that the past, present, and future are all occurring simultaneously at different frequencies.** All lifetimes are available as reflections of the one, the Light.

7. **In the Practice of the Night, as you lie down to sleep, you meditate on a symbol or mantra, and continue to do so throughout the entire night.** The primary focus is awareness and mindfulness. By maintaining focus on a mantra or visualization, you will naturally develop lucidity as a result of the increased awareness.

Unconscious Review Of Chapter 7

By now, you all know well enough that you have a conscious mind and an unconscious mind...not to mention a higher conscious mind...that serves as your guide to new learnings. As you are reading this...with all three minds... you probably have not fully considered just how well aligned they are at this very moment...and if you would perhaps, just stop for a moment, and fully consider now what the sign is that lets you know...in no uncertain terms that ***alignment*** is occurring...***within***. What would let you know inner alignment *is **increasing***...especially if you have been practicing...dreaming...while on the nightshift?

Now only you and your unconscious truly know for sure that once you have experienced lucidity...when the conscious mind wakes up to the other reality...and you know how to ***be*** lucid...that there is even more beyond that...such as becoming one with the Light...the Light from within and...without...conscious thought. In fact, how do we really know now that we are not already *ONE* with the light...which creates us, sustains us, protects us, and surrounds us? Because it is only our conscious mind that limits our experience of it, all the while our higher conscious mind is just waiting to assist us in experiencing it more fully...so, as the conscious mind may now be wondering how it is possible to experience the Light more deeply...it can be reminded of how important awareness, presence, and mindfulness are as you go along this path... especially while sleeping and meditating or doing a mantra throughout the night...to increase mindfulness...because when it comes down to it...it is only when you become **aware** of the Light...that you are! ***Fully*** consider that...and enjoy until we meet somewhere on the dream plane!

Dreamtime Interlude 1

Reality Testing:
Is This A Dream?

One of the fundamental skills which ultimately bridges the gap between "waking" reality and "dreaming" reality is knowing the difference between the two states. This might seem obvious during the waking state: that this reality is different from the one we live while we are dreaming. It may be a different story altogether when we "try" to recognize the same distinction while we are in the dream state. In the latter case we need to be aware of the fact that we are in a dream, while we are actually in the dream and asleep. One of the best ways to remember we are in a dream when we are, is to experience, discriminate, and label the difference between a night dream and waking reality.

The reality test is to sharpen our groundedness to Cartesian reality. Even though most people are hypnotized by, and mired exclusively into, this reality, they may not have an appreciation of its value. There are times when this reality works, times when it does not, and times when it limits our thinking. The more we become discriminating in understanding our reality from a scientific point of view, the easier it becomes to know when we are radically outside its realm. The reality test exercise helps us to develop this valuable skill. It is critical, scientific thinking applied to conscious, waking reality.

Literally the reality test asks, "Is this a dream?" In this way, we learn how we create rules for what is real and what is not. The New-Agers might really object to developing this kind of thinking. "Why not just trust your experience?" they might ask. "Isn't the idea to get out of our heads and into our experience?" Yes, that is exactly what we need to do. But first we need to define the boundaries of experience. Where are the boundaries between our ordinary, waking states and our dreaming realities or other mystical-type states? In *The Art Of Dreaming* (1993), Carlos Castenada's teacher, don Juan, on numerous occasions implores Carlos not to give in to "indulgences" when he is exploring alternate realities. Unpleasant experiences can result from indulgences in any state. However, when we are several realities away from consensual waking-state reality, the stakes are much greater if we are not disciplined. Using the reality strategy is one way of developing this discipline.

When we are in a night dream, it is so easy to be swept up into the dream reality and not even know it. It takes a fair amount of precision and energy to break through the dream trance and maintain clarity in that reality—to really be at choice. While we develop this critical ability, many other positive benefits and connections are being made at the unconscious level. Each time we ask ourselves "Is this a dream?" we are building a consistent chain of experiences in the waking state which refers to the dreaming state. The content of the backdrop, or dreamscape, comprises mostly twenty-four-hour day residue. These are the people, places, and things that we have experienced earlier in the day. The more we ask the question in our waking state, the more likely we are to develop the memory in our dream state. The idea is to develop the ability to ask this same question in our dream state. It is one of the easiest and most effective ways to become lucid. That is why we are introducing this now so you can ***begin practicing it***.

For some people, especially those who test out as "perceivers" on the Myers-Briggs Type Inventory, this may not be so easy to do in the beginning! This is because perceivers are so willing to adapt while they are in a dream. Ordinarily they do not stop and think that because something is bizarre, they must be in a dream. Our experience indicates that "judgers" (Myers-Briggs Type Inventory) have a greater likelihood of being lucid dreamers because of their ability to make fine distinctions and to evaluate them in different arenas. Stanford dream researcher Steven LaBerge and British psychologist Paul Tholey agree that the ability to really make fine, perceptual discriminations is fundamental to dreaming practices. This type of sensing and thinking is what most of us would call scientific, critical, Cartesian thinking, often characterized as dominant-hemispheric functioning. Later on in the book we will suggest that there are many limitations to thinking only in this linear, Cartesian way: like becoming ambidextrous, developing both sides provides the most choice.

On a biochemical level, reality testing helps to voluntarily activate the release of the neurotransmitter, norepinephrine, in the brain. In order to carry out higher dreaming practices, like lucid dreaming, we need to learn to control the chemical tides in our bodies with intention.

The Technique

There are three steps for reality testing and these are to be done as frequently as possible during waking hours.

1. **Ask yourself, "Is this a dream, right now?" or ask, "Am I dreaming?"** Then answer the question (without waxing philosophical!). Hint: the answer ought to be "no." That is the answer we want because we need to establish clear boundaries between daytime activity and nighttime activity.

2. **Ask yourself, "How do I know right now that I am in my waking state as opposed to my dream state?"** "How do I actually know?" Here we are looking for "dream signs."Certain "signs" or markers of reality in waking life are different from the signs of reality in dreaming life. What is it you can or cannot do now, that you can or cannot do when you are dreaming? What distinguishes the two different realities? Here are a few examples.

Waking Signs	Dreaming Signs
chair feels solid	chair melts, bends
jump into air—return to ground	jump into air—fly
change locations—clock time	change locations instantly
scene changes sequentially	scene changes automatically
"normal" color spectrum	black & white, vivid colors

3. **Ask yourself, "What would be happening differently if this were a dream?"** Answer this question with your unique dream signs. Consider what the reality test would look like if you blended in dream imagery. One of the most effective means for doing this is not just to imagine it, but to actually physically act out the dream sign, if possible. By putting the dream sign into physical operation you can experientially determine if you are dreaming or not.

   For example: when I jump in my waking state, I come back down to the ground. When I am in a dream at night, when I jump I can fly. So in this step of the reality test I jump and notice what happens. If I land on the ground I have experiential evidence that I am not dreaming! As crazy as it may sound, there will be a time in the future when you will go through the motions and carry out a reality test expecting nothing, and then you will jump...and you will fly...and you will become aware that you are in a dream while you are dreaming! That is how surprising it will be the first few times you become lucid.

To review, first ask:

1. **"Is this a dream, right now?"** Then always answer it. The answer will be "no" when you are in the waking state.
2. **"How do I know I am not dreaming?"** Answer this with your own real life experience.
3. **"What would be happening differently if this were a dream?"**

Complete these steps frequently throughout the day. If you are really serious, ten to fifteen times a day would be an excellent start.

Dreamtime Interlude 2

Getting To Know Your Unconscious Mind

One of the best ways to get to know your unconscious mind is to communicate with it. One of the easiest ways to communicate with the unconscious mind is by using a pendulum. Depending on your background with hypnosis or metaphysics this may trigger various associations.

We can assure you that pendulums have, indeed, made it out of the "dark ages." In the past twenty` years or so a number of credible writers, researchers, and clinicians have proposed using a pendulum as a way to activate what are known as "ideomotor signals." This idea is not a new one. The ideodynamic model of hypnosis was first proposed by Bernheim in the late 1800s (*Suggestive Therapeutics,* 1886). This and more recent models suggest that for every internal representation, there is a corresponding set of neural networks activated as a consequence of that thought. Think of a wonderful time you spent with someone special...begin to relive the experience, noticing how enjoyable it is...and notice how it automatically brings a smile to your face! Psychologist Leslie LeCron (*Journal Of Clinical Experimental Hypnosis,* 1954) and obstetrician David Cheek (Rossi & Cheek, 1988) have performed considerable clinical research expanding this idea using the pendulum.

You have heard of biofeedback, a process developed by researchers in physiological psychology. It operates on the principle that we are capable of consciously controlling so-called involuntary or automatic responses such as muscle tension and movement, heart rate, brain-wave frequencies and galvanic skin response if we are given the proper feedback. The "proper feedback" is through machines that measure, for example, our muscle tension and translate it into colored light: red for tension; green for mild relaxation; and blue for deep relaxation. The subject is told to change the color of the light. The light provides the conscious mind with amplified feedback about what the unconscious mind (the body, in this case) is doing. Most good biofeedback instruments are quite expensive. But here is the good news: you can use a pendulum to do the same thing. The pendulum is the most inexpensive biofeedback instrument available and it is much easier to use!

Researchers have found that when questions are directed to the body, or unconscious mind, it can respond through ideomotor movements. These movements are quite involuntary and subtle, yet the pendulum can detect and amplify these subtle movements so they can be seen consciously. This principle is intrinsic to the field of kinesiology and to the effectiveness of lie detectors or polygraphs. When a question is asked, both a verbal, conscious response and a physical response are registered to answer it. In other words, using a pendulum builds a bridge between the conscious and the unconscious minds, ultimately clearing the way for messages from the higher conscious mind.

Preparing To Communicate With Your Unconscious Mind

First, you need a pendulum. There are a couple of things you should look for when you buy or make one. Be sure that the chain is approximately six to eight inches long and the ball, pendant, or crystal at the bottom is not too light. If the chain is very long, very short, or if the pendulum is too light, the ideomotor responses will be too small for clear detection.

The technique you are about to carry out will enable you to elicit "yes," "no," and "not ready to consciously know, yet" responses. You are setting up a direct link with your unconscious mind. The third response is very important. It is common for the unconscious mind to be willing to do something, but only outside of conscious awareness, to preserve the integrity of the total personality. Allow it that latitude. Trying to make information conscious when it ought to remain unconscious will not support rapport between your conscious mind and unconscious mind. If you show respect and trust, it will often pleasantly surprise you with its sincerity and ingenuity.

Before you actually begin the series of exercises in this interlude, make sure that you are in a quiet place free of interruption, where you have some time for yourself. Rest your elbow comfortably on the arm of a chair or on a table.

The Technique

1. **Hold the pendulum so it is not moving and keep your hand still.** Hold the pendulum chain between your thumb and forefinger so that it is comfortable, and position your forearm so that you are looking at the pendulum down and in front of you. Look at the pendulum. Keep your eyes open, unless otherwise directed in the exercises.

2. **Ask for a "yes" response**. Ask the unconscious mind, *"Please swing the pendulum in a particular direction to indicate a 'yes' response."* Stop the pendulum when you observe a discernable, consistent direction. Thank your unconscious mind.
3. **Direct the unconscious to signal a "no" response**. Say, *"Please swing the pendulum in a different or opposing direction for a 'no' response."*Stop the pendulum when you have observed a discernable, consistent direction. Thank your unconscious mind.

4. **Direct the unconscious mind to signal a "not ready to consciously know, yet."** Say, *"Please swing the pendulum in some other way to indicate 'not ready to consciously know, yet.'"*

5. **Verify responses**. Just politely direct the unconscious mind to signal a "yes," "no," and "not ready to consciously know, yet." Make sure you stop the pendulum between responses. Language is important—if you ask the unconscious, "Could you give me a 'no' response?" it could answer "yes" it can!

If you experiment and ask your unconscious mind questions through a pendulum, remember to keep them simple, direct as possible, and binary in nature. Binary questions are yes/no questions. Each time you use your pendulum it is good to establish "yes," "no," and "not ready to know consciously, yet." Although many people find that these signals stay constant over time, we have also known them to change.

Additionally, when you ask your questions and experiment, be mindful that your unconscious mind is most accurate with its information about the past and present. Responses about the future lie in the domain of the higher conscious mind. This means that your unconscious mind could give you responses that it knows you want because it wants to please you. So have fun and explore.

The next two Interludes are also for your unconscious mind. They will be valuable tools for transformation as we proceed along the dream path.

Dreamtime Interlude 3

Unconscious Review And Integration For Dream Practices

The following exercise is designed to activate associations of memories, skills, abilities, and other resources that will assist you in your dreaming practices. The process is written so that you can insert any area of study for which you may want to prepare. For example, you can use this to activate resources that would assist you in remembering your dreams, dreaming lucidly, or for that matter any other abilities: psychic, spiritual or otherwise. It is a protocol that we have used in our Hypnosis III courses with excellent results.

It is important to recognize that ***your unconscious mind can review memories and representations outside your conscious awareness***. If you have never worked with your unconscious mind, this may seem like an unfamiliar concept—if that is the case, you are about to learn something that will make your life much easier. Your unconscious mind, as we mentioned in the review at the end of chapter 1, is capable of carrying out a multitude of tasks outside your awareness. Think of healing a cut, for example. Your unconscious mind knows how to heal your body. You do not have to know or be conscious of the processes it is mediating in your immune system, brain, endocrine system, and so on, in order for it to do its job effectively. It stores the information and activates it at the appropriate time.

The exercise you are about to do is a way of activating specific information to progress in your dreaming practices. It actually teaches you how to use the same process of activation, consolidation, and integration that would normally be done in your dreams, as we discussed in chapter 2. In that way you are also developing the ability to control the brain biochemistry necessary to progress to more advanced dreaming practices.

The Technique

1. **Establish ideomotor signals**. "Yes," "no," and "not ready to know consciously, yet." If you get a "not ready to consciously know, yet" response at any point, ask if it is okay to proceed sand to do the work outside your conscious awareness. Half of the fun of receiving this response is looking forward to being pleasantly surprised later on at what your unconscious mind has done!
2. **Create alignment and motivation**. *"Does my **unconscious know now** that finding and activating my internal resources to* (identify dream practice) *is important to me?"* If you get a "no" response, then explain to your unconscious mind precisely why dreaming practices are important to you. Be nice to it. Talk to it as you would a child of your own whom you love very much. Then ask the alignment and motivation question again.
3. **Unconscious search and review.**
   a) *"Will you, the unconscious mind, review the most important and formative events which, upon review, will deepen my ability to* (identify dream practice)*?"*
   b) *"As soon as you, the unconscious mind, have reached the first important event, signal with a 'yes' response."*
   c) *"And how much more comfortable and curious can I become while you, the unconscious mind, reviews this event?"*
   d) *"I would like you, the unconscious mind, to review three more events or series of events which you believe to be the most important and formative ones. You can signal with a 'yes' when you begin your review, and you can signal later with a 'yes' when you end."*
   e) *"Is there anything else that you, the unconscious would like to review to fully prepare me for* (identify dreaming practice)*?"* If you get a "no," or a "not ready to consciously know, yet" go on to step 4. If you get a"yes," review that information and then go on to step 4.
4. **Reorient**. Close your eyes and ask your unconscious, *"Open my eyes only after you, the unconscious, have fully integrated the learnings from the review, so that I can be refreshed, relaxed and alert."*

Dreamtime Interlude 4

Using Unconscious Interviewing For Clearing
...The Way To Your Dreaming Practices

This technique can be used at any point in your dreaming practices when an unwanted emotion, belief, or conflict surfaces. It is a safe and effective way to gain access to state-bound information in order to accelerate personal development. It is an excellent way to complete issues revealed in the dream interpretation covered in chapter 5 (or any other issues that may come as a course of being a human being).

One important point here: it is not important whether you actually have conscious recall of any of the information coming from the unconscious mind. It is important that you use the experience to develop trust in your unconscious mind and develop the conviction that there is more to you than you think. If you begin to encounter uncomfortable emotions or become confused at any point while carrying out this technique, we suggest that you stop the procedure immediately and consult a professional hypnotherapist, counselor or psychologist in your area..

We have also taught this technique at our Hypnosis III course and have used it ourselves when we have encountered blocks. One example that comes to mind is when I used this technique to develop my intuitive abilities related to working with my dreams. Whenever I would think about carrying out more advanced dreaming practices, I would feel discouraged and begin thinking, "I will never be able to do this," and lose my motivation. When I asked my unconscious mind to *find that event or series of events that, when reviewed, will resolve the problem,* I was surprised to remember something that I had not thought about consciously since the time it happened.

> *I was about four years old. I awakened very early one morning, just before dawn. As I looked across my bed I saw a white shadowy figure suspended in front of a closed closet door on the other side of the room. I was sure it was a ghost.*

I was not scared. In fact, I was curious and intrigued. I watched for a while and it just hovered there. I am not sure what happened after that, but I remember falling back asleep. When I woke up an hour or two later the shadowy figure was gone. It was a Saturday morning, and I could hear both of my parents in the kitchen, so I scampered out to the kitchen and excitedly announced that I had seen a ghost. After a brief discussion, they told me that it was just one of my father's white shirts hanging on the doorknob of the closet in my room. I remember feeling confused and disappointed. "It seemed so real," I thought, "and it was much higher than a shirt hanging from the door." But I knew my parents always tried to help me and would not say anything that they did not really believe, so I believed them. I decided at that point that I could not trust what I saw (or later what I would call my intuition or psychic abilities). Just through the realization of the memory, I knew what I needed to learn from it, "That it is okay to trust my intuition." When I got to the healing phase, all I could feel was warm feelings about myself and my parents. A short time later, I made a leap in my lucid dreaming.

Now, we are not suggesting that you will have as powerful an experience as that every time you use this process. What we are suggesting, though, is that each time you use it, you will increase your alignment with your unconscious mind. Remember, your unconscious mind holds the keys. It interprets and symbolizes all of the information that your higher conscious mind transmits to you. What it believes to be true or what it feels, will largely dictate what conscious experience you have...of anything. Consult with it, makes friends with it, and it will be your greatest ally in this life.

The Technique

1. **Define the problem and the outcome.**
   Problem: What is the challenge, obstacle, or block that is in the way?
   Outcome: What is it that you want? How do you want to be different?
   Make sure that your outcome is positively stated as something you want. In other words if you have something like "I want to clear this block to remembering my dream," or "I do not want to have fear about...," in both cases you will need to say what you *do* want. For example, "I want to remember my dreams," or "I want to feel confident about doing dreaming practices."

2. **Establish ideomotor signals**. "Yes," "no," and "not ready to consciously know, yet."

3. **Create alignment and motivation**. *"Does my **unconscious know now** that* (outcome and/or resolution of the problem) *is important to me?"* If you receive a "no" response, then explain to your unconscious mind, precisely why dreaming practices are important to you. Be nice to it. Talk to it as you would a child of your own whom you love very much. Then ask the alignment and motivation question again.

4. **Unconscious search and review.**
   a) *"Will you, my unconscious mind, find that event or series of events that, when reviewed, will resolve the problem?"* (If you receive a "no," ask if it will do it completely outside of your awareness in a way that will keep you safe and comfortable.)
   b) *"As soon as you, my unconscious mind, reach the event or series of events, you can signal with a 'yes' response."*
   c) *"And how much more comfortable and curious can I become while you, my unconscious mind, review this event?"* (You can suggest repeated reviewing, if necessary, and have the unconscious mind signal each time it begins and each time it ends a review.)

5. **Suggestion for conscious recall and discussion**. *"And when you, my unconscious mind, have an important insight, learning, or thought that you want me to consciously consider, will you just let it bubble up into my awareness only to the extent necessary to achieve* (outcome)*?"* If you get a "yes" then ask it for the insight. Often the insight will just bubble up without the "yes" response. If you get a "no" or "not ready to consciously know, yet," ask if it will store and activate the insight or learning outside your awareness.

6. **Facilitate unconscious healing**. *"When you, my unconscious mind, are ready let me go into a deeper state of healing to complete this change, you can close my eyes, and then open my eyes after you have completed the healing for now."*

Dreamtime Interlude 5

Getting To Know Your Higher Conscious Mind

The following is a simple meditation to de-identify with the aspects of ourselves which have the potential for limiting us. In identifying strongly with certain aspects (such as our intellect, our body, or our age) we can limit who and what we are. When we limit ourselves through our beliefs we can also limit our access to higher realms. For example, if our conscious mind denies the existence of a higher conscious mind then we will not have conscious experience of its role in our life. Since our higher conscious mind is our connection to greater realms of existence, we will only experience these realms to the degree that we believe in the power of the higher conscious mind.

This process begins with a few minutes of conscious breathing. The most appropriate breath for the purpose of this meditation is to exhale twice as long as you inhale. In other words, the ratio of the inhalation to the exhalation is one to two. This breath automatically activates your parasympathetic nervous system, otherwise known as the "relaxation response." It will produce a state of relaxed alertness. You want to breathe long enough to have a sense of this relaxed alertness and the accompanying movement of energy throughout your body. Then begin the next phase of the meditation.

Do each line of the meditation slowly enough to have time to comprehend the meaning. In other words, do it with the same commitment as the reality test, so you are fully considering what you are thinking. If you would like to, continue the breathing while you go through the words; or, if it is easier in the beginning, allow your breathing to return to normal while reciting them and then return to the 1:2 ratio for a few moments between each line. After you have completed the last line you can either continue to repeat it or just breathe and notice what happens.

Over time this meditation can be modified for special circumstances that may arise through your dreaming practices. If you are experiencing challenges with certain emotions or desires, begin your meditation with these. For example, "I have fear, but I am not my fear. I am more than my fear." This is an excellent way to de-identify with aspects of yourself that can sometimes seem larger than you—it puts these things in perspective. If, after doing the meditation, the emotion, belief, fixation, or identification still remains, use the clearing technique with the pendulum.

In the beginning, we suggest you use the meditation as it is here. We have used it and taught it to our students. Some report that they had been skeptical about the existence of a higher conscious mind and, through doing this meditation, have had experiences that verified its presence for them. We suggest you do this daily for five to ten minutes. It will begin to culture your neurology and prepare you for the Dreaming Meditation in the next Dreamtime Interlude.

The Meditation

I have a body, but I am not my body.
I am more than my body.

I have emotions, but I am not my emotions.
I am more than my emotions.

I have a conscious mind, but I am not my conscious mind.
I am more than my conscious mind.

I have an unconscious mind, but I am not my unconscious mind.
I am more than my unconscious mind.

I have dreams, but I am not my dreams.
I am more than my dreams.

I have thoughts, but I am not my thoughts.
I am more than my thoughts.

No matter what I think I am, I am always more than that...

Dreamtime Interlude 6

Dreaming Meditation Technique

This Dreaming Meditation Technique which we have developed has many aspects in common with other Eastern and Western Dream Traditions. It is an excellent meditation technique in and of itself. We will use it as a vehicle for incubation later. For now, we suggest that you practice this meditation at least once a day after you have completed the book. This is the second primary way that we will use to build bridges between consensual, waking state reality and the dream state. It is a valuable vehicle that we will use for the more advanced dreaming practices mentioned in the later part of this book. The state you will access while using this meditation will be very similar to REM sleep. This means that it is an excellent vehicle to transfer information from your waking state to your dreaming state.

The Technique

1. **Find a location to do your meditation**. This is a place where you can sit and be in touch with good feelings and your inner resources. We suggest that you find some convenient place in your home. We like to use our bed, since this meditation is directly associated with night-time dreams. A hint: if you use your bed, make sure that you sit up. Lying down, while being quite comfortable, will fire off all of your associations with sleep. The idea is to alter your state and have awareness!

2. **Hold a dream stone in your hand**. This step is optional, but has a lot of benefits, so we strongly suggest it. Find a small stone or crystal (if you like crystals), that is small enough to hold easily in your hand. In this step you can place it anywhere in your hand that is comfortable for you. In step 6 of this meditation, we will change the location of the stone, to use it as an anchor, or an unconscious reminder, to be in the Witness state (see the following pages).

3. **Focus on a point in front of you, above eye level**. Our advice is to always start your meditation this way to condition your neurology. This is generally the shortest step of the dreaming meditation. Take only the time you need to focus and center yourself before you proceed to the next step.

4. **Expand your awareness to include all of the space around, below, and above you**. Essentially, what you are doing in this state is switching from focused, foveal vision to peripheral vision. Peripheral vision is associated with parasympathetic arousal (the relaxed, alert state). Our experience with more than a thousand students and clients, as well as ourselves, suggests this is one of the quickest ways to enter a relaxed, meditative state that will block fight-and-flight states. It is well documented in many shamanic systems as a "doorway" state to mystical experiences. Many healers intuitively use this state. Most martial arts teach it. Many professional athletes use it naturally or have been trained to do so. In this procedure we suggest that you expand your awareness not only to the space along the sides, but also to the space below you and above you.

   The easiest way to shift into peripheral vision, while looking at the point on the wall, is to allow your eye muscles to relax. As your eyes soften, your vision may get slightly blurry. While keeping your eyes fixed, in soft focus on the point, expand your awareness to the front corners of the room or area. Continue to expand your awareness all the way to the space behind you, below you, and above you. You ought to notice a significant shift in your state of consciousness. Your facial muscles will usually become flaccid, your jaw relaxed, and your breathing will naturally lower. Most people experience not only expanded visual awareness, but also expanded auditory and kinesthetic awareness.

5. **Make the source of your attention about three inches down from the top of your head and two inches behind your eyes**. This is the approximate location of your pineal gland, a pea-like structure that hangs from your hypothalamus. It is the location of the third eye in the chakra system, the home of second sight and intuition. Western science believes that the pineal gland senses light-dark cycles, which are triggers for our circadian and ultradian rhythms.

6. **Move the source of your attention to about eighteen inches above the crown of your head, slightly behind you**. Simultaneously let the stone come to rest in a special, yet comfortable position in your hand; a position that will be easy to replicate in future meditations. This is the archetypical location of the Higher Self. Some traditions refer to it as the seat of Witness consciousness. Most people notice a subtle, but recognizable, difference among peripheral vision, pineal vision, and Witness vision.

7. **Reverse the steps to reorient to normal waking state**. As soon as you are about to float back down into the pineal position, shift the position of the stone back to where you were holding it in step 2. This means, for now, that you only hold the stone in the special position when you are in the Witness position.

The following is a "no frills" demonstration that we do in some of our seminars to give you an idea of how this goes.

John: ....So, **holding the stone** however you want right now, (and we will tell you when to put it in the other position that you have just selected)... So, here we go. Just go ahead and **find that point**.

Julie: On the wall.

John: And then as you do, go ahead and allow your eyes to soften.

Julie: **Just allow the muscles around your eyes, your face, just to relax.**

John: Notice a shift in your breathing.

Julie: Comfortably.

John: And begin to **allow your awareness to expand to the front corners of the room** all the while continuing to keep your eyes directed on the point on the wall.

Julie: So you can see the front right corner, the front left corner, and you can do that easily while your eyes maintain their focus on that point...

John: And then **allow your awareness to expand** all the way to the sides of the room. And then **to the space behind you**.

Julie: ...And continuing to **expand your awareness to the space above you and below you**.

John: All the while still keeping your eyes open, soft, staring at the point, awareness expanding. And then **focus the source of your awareness on a point that is behind your eyes...a few inches down from the top of your skull**. And then as you begin to notice that the source of your awareness is right at that point, where your pineal gland is, you can move that stone to the comfortable position you have decided to use. Just as that stone settles into the comfortable position, **then allow your awareness, the source of your awareness to move about eighteen inches above your head and slightly behind you.**

Julie: Notice you can just kind of float in space... so that you can easily have your awareness above your head, so you could look down on the top of your head and notice your hair, your shoulders, and look out past where your body is and just have an awareness of being up there, looking down on yourself, have your awareness up above, all the way up, right in that comfortable space. And as you do...

John: (at the same time as above) ...Maintaining peripheral vision, maintaining the awareness of the space around you...as awareness expands...comfortably...awareness... your source...your awareness...above you...expanding all around.

Julie: And if it suits you to do that with your eyes closed, if you have not already, just go right ahead and close your eyes and notice that space up there eighteen inches above, and just a little further back from the top of your head.... And just keep bringing your awareness back to that space above your head.

John: Awareness expanding...

Julie: While still perceiving what is around you, behind you, from the scope of being above so that you can have a sense of everything around you, below you, and even sense of what might be above you, above that space eighteen inches above your head.

John: Then, when you are ready...**begin to bring the source of your awareness back down to the point where your pineal gland is behind your eyes. Transfer the stone to some other place in your hand.**

Julie: Just bring your focus down and bring your awareness back inside your head.

John: While **your awareness remains expanded all the way out to the periphery**.... And when you are ready, allow your **eyes** to **open** while you still look ahead at that point you looked at before you started.

Julie: ....And come back out...comfortably...taking all the time you want...Hmmm...Nice state, isn't it?

Dreamtime Interlude 7

Moe Uhane:
The Hawaiian Dreamtime Chant

We thought that it would be fitting to close these Interludes with a chant that is very near and dear to us. It is one we have spent countless dreaming hours chanting, feeling, and being. This chant comes from our friends, Huna mentors, and chanting buddies, Tad James and Ardie Flynn who did the esoteric translation and taught us its "melody."

Moe Uhane

He kanaka loa
He kanaka poko
He ui aa he alaneo
A na maka pa i ka lani
Malu ka honua
Ia kama uhili e
Hee nei Ku
I ka moe au a ke kahuna

I call the Higher Self.
I call the Lower Self.
I dare to make a call all the way to the Alaneo.
Make (touch) the close connection with the Guides from the Supreme Heavens.
Bring the protection, blessings all the way to me here on Earth.
Enter me through the mouth, braid, tie on. Make a close connection.
You change and transform me from a solid to a liquid (as in alchemy), and the Body/Mind vibration is raised up.
And I enter the Supreme meditation (sleep) with the aid of the Kahuna.

Glossary Of Terms

acetylcholine — (see "neurotransmitter") a neurotransmitter found widely throughout the body. Among its functions are slowing of the heart and rhythmic stimulation of the digestive muscles after eating which together create a feeling of relaxation, as well as consolidation of learning during REM sleep. Acetylcholine was the first neurotransmitter to be discovered.

amine, acetylcholine — (see "neurotransmitter") the neurotransmitters responsible for activating sympathetic arousal or "fight or flight" states characterized by increased heart rate and blood and sugar and activation of circuits that control attention. Aminergic molecules are central to the process of encoding new information received by the nervous system.

anterior hypothalamus — (see "hypothalamus") front portion of the hypothalamus which directly mediates the restorative functions of sleep and digestion.

ARAS (Ascending Reticular Activating System) — portion of the brain stem which is responsible for waking functions such as rousing from sleep, attention and startle responses.

ashram — a guru's residence. Disciples may also inhabit an ashram which is considered a sacred space for intentional community living. Meditation, chanting, and yoga are frequent daily activities in Hindu-inspired ashrams.

avatar — a fully realized master; an ascended being who enters an incarnation already enlightened. Some would say that avatars are living examples of God itself. They come into the world to bring love, light and healing; they also counterbalance the less positive forces.

bardos intermediate states of consciousness as defined by *The Tibetan Book Of The Dead* and the Dzogchen School of Buddhism. There are said to be six bardos to transcend along the path—ranging from everyday, consensual reality to choosing the next incarnation.

basic rest activity cycle (BRAC) Nathaniel Kleitman's model of fluctuating cycles of arousal and motor behavior that recur approximately every 90-100 minutes; he first observed these cycles in animals and then later in humans. He then discovered, along with Eugene Aserinski, that BRAC was related to an internal rhythm in the human body, now known as the ultradian rhythm.

binary questions based on bivalent logic where every statement is true/false. These questions require an either/or answer rather than a choice of answers along the continuum. Yes/no questions are binary, as compared to open-ended questions which allow many possible answers.

brain waves bio-electrical waves or signals which occur in the brain. They were first measured by Hans Berger. These waves can be measured by an electroencephalogram (EEG) in units of cycles per second. There are four generally accepted levels of EEG patterns:
beta: 13 c.p.s. and above
alpha: 8-12 c.p.s.
theta: 4-7 c.p.s.
delta: 1-3 c.p.s.

Cartesian reality Rene Descartes' philosophy of dualism which divides the world into an objective world of matter (the domain of science) and a subjective world of mind (the domain of religion). He proposed that objects are separate and distinct from consciousness. According to Descartes, an observer could witness any "external" event and not influence it through the process of observation. The scientific method is based on this philosophy.

chakras, chakra system from Hinduism and Buddhism. A system of non-material, psychic vortices, or centers, found at specific locations within the human body. Each chakra has specific spiritual, mental, emotional and physical functions. There are generally considered to be seven major chakras:
first chakra—base of spine—basic bodily functions, instinct, survival
second chakra—reproductive organs—sexual functions,unconscious processes, creativity
third chakra—solar plexus—digestion, power and activity
fourth chakra—heart—cross-over of body and spirit, love
fifth chakra—throat—speech and hearing, self-expression
sixth chakra—"third eye"—light/dark cycles, intuitive insight, clairvoyance
seventh chakra—"crown" of head—connection to higher spiritual realms

cholines (see "neurotransmitter") neuro-modulators and the family of neurotransmitters responsible for the relaxation response.

conscious mind (see "unconscious mind", "higher conscious mind") one's present awareness; reflexive consciousness which functions in an intellectual, analytical manner to direct one's voluntary actions. The conscious mind contrasts with the unconscious mind which does things automatically and intuitively *outside* one's awareness.

corpus callosum the dense nerve bundle bridge which allows transmission of electro-chemical impulses between the brain's hemispheres.

cortex, cerebral cortex the outer layer of the brain which is most highly developed in humans. Responsible for higher functions such as language, reason, perception of patterns and symbols, and the development of our culture.

circadian rhythms the body's basic 24+/-0.5 hour (one-day) cycle, its internal clock, which corresponds to light and dark cycles in nature.

dream incubation the process of seeding dreams in a purposeful way to accomplish some goal or objective. Before going to sleep, one gives the unconscious mind a directive to dream in a way that supports a specific outcome. For example, "What would be an interesting way for me to begin my presentation tomorrow? Unconscious mind, please dream the answer so it is clear to me when I awaken."

dreamscape the inner landscape of the mind which is present during dreaming. The scenery, the backdrop, the people and objects that are part of the dream itself.

Dreamtime, the the concept of reality—waking reality and dreaming reality—as being THE one ultimate all-inclusive reality that is beyond time, space, and matter.

dream yoga the practice of creating "union" (yoga) with the source, or achieving enlightenment through dreams. Its purpose is to "wake up" to one's true divine nature.

Dzogchen Practice of the Clear (Natural) Light Dzogchen is a sect of Tantric Tibetan Buddhism which practices dream yoga, known as the Practice of the Clear or Natural Light. Dream yoga is practiced at the moment of falling asleep and before entering the dream state. The Clear Light, according to Dzogchen, is the innate, natural luminosity that manifests in its fullest expression in the state after death. Dzogchen believe that each of us has within a droplet of light (the Son Light) that is part of an undivided sea of light (the Mother Light). Through correct meditation one can transcend and full recognise the Clear Light during this life, to integrate with the Mother Light after the death of one's physical body.

EEG (Electro-encephalogram — a machine which measures electrical activity in the form of brain waves by placing electrodes on the scalp and measuring voltage. To this day the exact location of the source of the signals within the brain is unknown. Rather the EEG waves are indications of activity in generalized areas of the brain.

electron — sub-atomic building block of matter which carries a negative charge but has no mass. An electron can behave as a wave or particle depending on the method of measurement. As a wave its location is uncertain. As a particle, its momentum is uncertain. It behaves like an amorphous sphere, but unlike most spheres it has to rotate 720 degrees (not 360 degrees) to make one full revolution!

engram — a memory trace. A specific site or location of the brain which contains specific memory. The notion of the engram was largely supported by the work of Walter Penfield, an esteemed Canadian neurosurgeon in the 1920s. Beginning with the research of Karl Lashley, it has been demonstrated that memory is not located in any one site but, rather, is organised more along functional lines. With the discovery of neurotransmitters, it is now believed that memory is stored holographically throughout the community cells of the body through configurations of electro-chemical waves.

explicate — (see "implicate") quantum physicist David Bohm's label for the domain referred to as "Cartesian reality"; the three dimensional, material reality which is rooted in space/time locations. It is characterized by separate entities which can be observed or measured. It is secondary to a higher, organizing order—the implicate—which enfolds to manifest the explicate reality. The explicate is the material reality that is created when consciousness interacts with the implicate order.

foveal vision — one of two types of vision capable in the human eye. Foveal vision is detailed, tunnel vision controlled by the cones on the center of the eye's retina.

frequency domain — the entire field, or universe, which is composed of interference patterns of waves. It is the entire field of all possibilities. Synonymous with the implicate order, the Void, and the quantum field. Literally, beyond words.

galvanic skin response — scientific electrical measurement of the amount of perspiration changes (moisture) on the surface of the skin. Often used as a basic indicator of stress and/or relaxation. The greater the amount of moisture, the higher the level of stress, and vice versa.

higher conscious mind or higher self — (see "conscious mind", "unconscious mind") one's guide and connection to higher realms of spirit. The divine in the human, it functions in a loving, protective way and guides one through dreams, intuitions, and creativity. It is the drop of light that is a part of an undivided sea of light, known as the Son Light of Dzogchen.

hologram — (see "holographic") a three-dimensional, visual representation that is created when a laser beam is split into two beams. One beam is bounced off the object to be photographed. Another beam is directed to collide with the reflected light of the first beam, which then creates an interference pattern of light waves. This interference pattern is recorded on a piece of film which is called a holographic plate. What is striking about the holographic plate is that if it is broken into pieces, each piece, when light is passed through it, will project the original object contained in the whole picture. This phenomenon inspired David Bohm to create a holographic theory of the universe.

holographic (see "hologram") model of reality, generally credited to David Bohm, in which each part of the whole contains the whole within itself (with somewhat lesser detail). Based on the metaphor of the hologram. Applied to the universe, it suggests that even the smallest piece of the universe, a sub-atomic particle, is representative of the entire universe as an undivided whole. They both represent a multi-dimensional enfolded reality. In many ancient, metaphysical systems this notion is expressed by the maxim, "as above, so below."

Huna literally translates as "the secret." Huna is the ancient Hawaiian system of psychology, philosophy, and spiritualism, which is sometimes referred to as religion. In Huna, there are three gods: the conscious mind "Lono;" the unconscious mind "Ku;" and the higher conscious mind "Kane." The Hawaiians used mana, or life force energy, to bring alignment so these three minds worked harmoniously together.

hypnogogic state relaxed, trance-like state which occurs just prior to the onset of sleep. It is characterized by seemingly random, stream-of-consciousness thoughts and images.

hypnopompic state relaxed, trance-like state which occurs just after awakening from sleep, prior to any gross body movements. Excellent time for autosuggestion.

hypothalamus command centre in the brain responsible for food intake, endocrine levels, water balance, sexual rhythms and autonomic nervous system functioning. It is the central switchboard for motivation states.

ideomotor movements, ideomotor signals repetitive, often barely visible, micro-muscle movements which correspond to mental representations. These movements when amplified and systematically utilized become signals from the unconscious mind/body. Ideomotor signals, used in conjunction with binary "yes"/"no" questioning, facilitate reliable and direct communication with the unconscious mind. A common approach is to use the pendulum for amplifying micro-muscle movements in the hand and arm to demonstrate "yes"/"no" responses.

impeccability a term from the Toltec spiritual system, as described by Carlos Casteneda and his teacher don Juan Matus, to signify the economical, efficient and precise use of energy for any given task. According to the Toltec tradition, it is a yardstick of personal evolution. The opposite of impeccability in this system is indulgence. Indulgence is the reckless, imprecise use of energy.

implicate (see "explicate") Bohm's label for the basic order from which our three dimensional reality is created. It is the enfolded, multidimensional, frequency domain of pure potentiality. This potential unfolds into the material world (the explicate order) when it interacts with consciousness (observation). In spiritual texts, what Bohm describes as the "implicate order" is referred to as the Unmanifest Manifest, the Void (Buddhist), the I'o (Hawaiian), the Akasha (Hindu), to name a few. Bohm and his collaborator, Hindu saint, Jiddu Krishnamurti, contend that this subtle level of reality can only be known implicitly (primarily through meditation), hence the term, implicate. Any attempt to experience it through the external senses or describe it (which are functions of the explicate) limits its boundless scope.

kahuna literally translates as "keeper" (kahu) of the "secret" (huna). An expert in a recognized discipline (akin to a PhD) within the Hawaiian spiritual system, known as Huna. There are kahunas, or experts, in astronomy, canoe building, agriculture, herbs, medicine, dreams, hula, etc.

karma (law of) spiritual law which suggests that actions have a collective effect on the results of one's life. In Hindu philosophy, karma is cumulative from incarnation to incarnation and is a major determinant of the content of each lifetime. It is the underlying message of the Biblical adage, "As you sow, so shall you reap."

kinesiology commonly referred to as "muscle testing". A system for asking questions and using the body to derive answers from the relative strength or weakness of the muscle responses after a question has been asked. It is another method of accessing unconscious responses as they are communicated through the body. Similar to ideomotor signalling.

kinesthetic mantra (see "mantra") a kinesthetic mantra refers to the use of a sensation to focus or absorb one's consciousness. For example, physically holding a stone as one falls asleep, and continuing to hold it throughout the night, is one way to maintain consciousness through periods of deep sleep and dreaming.

lucid dreaming the ability to be consciously aware of being in a dream while dreaming; to "wake up" in a dream while still remaining physically asleep. May be used as a spiritual practice to attain enlightenment.

mana the Hawaiian word meaning "life force energy." The concept of energy was central to Hawaiian spirituality.

mantra a repetitive word, or sound, used in the practice of meditation. The word or sound may be given by a guru, a teacher, or the practitioner may select their own word or sound. The mantra is then repeated for a period of time to create transcendence.

maya cosmic illusion. The Hindu term referring to the veil of illusion which man must pierce to realize he is one with the source, the light, God. In quantum physics terms, the explicate order, our everyday perception of the material world, is maya. It is the veil which clouds our direct perception (beyond our senses) of the true nature of reality and Self.

mind-body controversy the debate also known as the mind-body split. Originated in the 17th century through an agreement between Descartes and the Roman Catholic Church wherein they created the notion that the mind and body were two separate entities, each having little effect on the other. This agreement laid strict boundaries of demarcation: making mind (synonymous with soul at that time) the domain of the Church and the body the domain of physicians and scientists. Modern medicine is based upon this split. With the advent of psychosomatic medicine in the 1930s and psychoneuroimmunology (PNI) in the past twenty years, scientists are now acknowledging the interconnectedness of the mind and body. It is now becoming increasingly accepted that the mind and body function as an interdependent, undivided whole.

Myers-Briggs Type inventory a personality inventory widely utilized in business and psychology to profile personal typology and to predict behaviour; developed by Isabella Briggs-Myers. It is based upon the psychological types originally proposed and developed by Carl Jung in 1923. It profiles individuals according to four scales: introvert-extrovert, intuitor-sensor, thinker-feeler, and judger-perceiver. The judger-perceiver scale determines how one adapts to one's environment.

judger: functions well in an environment of planned orderliness.

perceiver: functions well in an open-ended, flexible environment of moment-to-moment responses.

new physics — quantum physics as prosposed by Heisenberg and s in the early 1900s as differentiated from Newtonian physics ("classical" physics which was developed in the 17th century). Quantum physics theory is a comprehensive, mathematical theory explaining the behaviour of systems. It is based on the idea that discrete energy packets (quanta) leap or make discontinuous transitions. Essentially, it suggests that individual events within a system are uncertain, unpredictable, non-separable, and observer-dependent. A lot to think about!

non-lucid dream — (see "lucid dreaming") a dream in which the dreamer does not consciously awaken and become lucid. Most dreams are non-lucid. In non-lucid dreams, the dreamer is unaware of being in a dream and therefore makes no discrimination about whether the dream is "real" or whether it is similar to, or different from, waking consensual reality.

norepinephrine (noradrenaline) — a neurotransmitter in the amine family largely responsible for temperature regulation, and therefore, waking attention and emotional states. At night typically there are much lower norepinephrine levels. For lucid dreaming to occur there needs to be higher concentrations of norepinephrine (in order to "wake up" while in a dream while the body is still asleep). Lucid dreaming practices literally enable the dreamer to voluntarily secrete norepinephrine, as well as other neurotransmitters.

neuromodulators — a specific class of neurotransmitters which have longer time-course actions which set a chemical "tide" in the nervous system; the tide then facilitates widespread excitation of certain neurons and the inhibition of others. For example, during sleep cholinergic neuromodulators (choline tides) make it difficult for certain aminergic (waking) neurotransmitters to be present in large quantities. Similarly, during our waking hours the aminergic neuromodulators (amine tides) inhibit the preponderance of certain cholinergic neurotransmitters.

neuropeptide the chemical messengers, made of amino acids, which the body uses to communicate with its cells, tissues, organs, etc. Originally they were called "neuro"peptides because they were first discovered in the brain and nervous system. Later scientists discovered them throughout the entire body but by then the name was in common usage, so it remains.

neurotransmitter a chemical substance which transmits nerve impulses across synapses (gaps) between neurons. They are often referred to as "chemical communicators" because they carry information between cells throughout the entire nervous system. For example, dopamine is a neurotransmitter and is one of the amines comprising the amine tides; acetylcholine, also a neurotransmitter, is one of the cholines comprising the choline tides.

parallel universe a theory first conceived in 1957 by Hugh Everett III, a Princeton University physicist. He posited that quantum physics predicted the existence of an infinite number of universes. As the universe, and each thing within it, is measured, it splits into as many universes (realities) as there are possibilities.

parasympathetic arousal the autonomic nervous system is divided into two parts: the parasympathetic arousal system and sympathetic arousal system. When the parasympathetic nervous system is activated it inhibits fight and flight states (sympathetic arousal). Parasympathetic arousal is correlated with the relaxation response.

particle — (see "wave") in physics, a particle usually denotes a very small piece of matter such as an atom (atomic particle) or electron (sub-atomic particle). An electron can appear as either a particle or a wave, depending on how the experiment is constructed. When it behaves as a particle, it occupies only one point of space at a time. When it acts as a wave, it spreads throughout space. In scientific observation, it is one or the other. The concept that matter can exist as either a wave or a particle but can be observed as both simultaneously is known as wave-particle duality.

peripheral vision — (see "foveal vision") the human eye has two types of vision: peripheral and foveal. Peripheral vision is controlled by the rods on the periphery of the retina of the eye. It is characterized by panoramic, expansive vision which is especially sensitive to movement and contour. Many mystical traditions use peripheral vision as a way to alter consciousness.

PGO (ponto-geniculo-occipital) waves — a characteristic EEG pattern during REM sleep:

pons: located in the brain stem, it is the site from which the neuromodulators flow, changing the states of consciousness back and forth between the amines and the cholines. The pons is a bridge between the cerebral cortex (responsible for reason, language) and the cerebellum (responsible for motor programs).

geniculo-occipital: a specific region in the occipital lobe responsible for interpretation of visual stimuli.

photon — the smallest unit of light energy. An electron of light. While measurable, a photon has no electrical charge or mass, although it is capable of creating a burst of momentum.

pineal gland a master gland responsible for the secretion of melatonin which regulates the circadian rhythm, or light/dark cycles. Believed by Descartes to be the seat of the soul. Until the 1980s, it was thought to be an atrophied gland with little importance. It is now recognized as a master gland which mediates the function of the pituitary and thyroid glands. Research has verified high levels of serotonin in the area of the pineal gland during psychic and spiritual visions and during the use of hallucinogenic substances. Esoterically, it is correlated with the third eye chakra.

pineal vision focusing awareness on the pineal gland and "seeing" the world from the point of view of being inside the pineal gland, looking outward. Meditation on the pineal gland is used in a number of mystical and spiritual systems.

positive internal representation a mental image, or thought, that is directed toward what is wanted, as opposed to what is not wanted. The unconscious mind is said to be quite literal and therefore does not easily handle negation. The word "not" exists only in language, not in our sensory-based reality. When one tries not to think of the word or colour "purple", for example, one has to think about it first. In goal-setting, often people focus on what they do not want, such as "I don't want to be overweight any more." In a positive internal representation, the focus is on what is desired. "I want to weigh a healthy 150 pounds." A positive internal representation, which is created mentally, is an image, a sound, words, a feeling, or a combination of these.

postural atonia the inhibition of the voluntary muscles during sleep. This prevents one from actually physically acting out dream content while asleep. For example, postural atonia prevents one from running around the bedroom while dreaming of running a race.

prefrontal lobe — the portion of the cerebral cortex just behind the forehead which is responsible for judgement, intention and reflexive consciousness. It is the most recently and highly evolved part of the cerebral cortex. During lucid dreaming, norepinephrine is secreted in the prefrontal lobe, resulting in the ability to become aware of being in the dream state.

REM (rapid eye movement) — repetitive micro-muscle movements of the eyes which occur approximately every 90-100 minutes and correlate with dreaming. REM was discovered in 1953 by Eugene Aserinski and Nathaniel Kleitman. During REM there are numerous biochemical changes that facilitate the consolidation of learning, the conversion of short-term to long-term memory, the testing and rehearsal of motor programs, as well as other psychological benefits.

second sight — psychic vision and /or clairvoyance, the ability to see hidden realms, guides, and auras. Second sight is the vision associated with the opening of the third eye (pineal gland).

serotonin — (see "neurotransmitter") a neurotransmitter which is present in a wide range of mental phenomena from sleep cycles, to psychosis, psychic visions, and hallucinogenic drug states. It is found in the highest concentrations in the pineal gland, but is also found throughout the rest of the body.

sleep cycle (non-REM/ REM cycle — each sleep cycle lasts approximately 90-100 minutes. The cycle is divided between non rapid eye movement (non-REM) and rapid eye movement (REM) sleep. Non-REM is divided into four stages: stages I, II, III and IV, according to the progressive change in the EEG to a high-voltage, slow-wave pattern. As the sleep cycle repeats itself throughout the night, the proportion of REM sleep increases and non-REM decreases.

sleep spindles, spindles, spindle waves waves which oscillate at 15-18 c.p.s., which generally mark the transition of stage I sleep to stage II sleep. In our waking state, spindles are associated with reading or dozing off at a lecture.

slow-wave sleep stages III and IV of sleep. Stage III sleep is defined by a mixture of sleep spindles with higher voltage readings than stage II and slower waves. Stage IV occurs as the spindles cease and the high-voltage (200 millivolts) slow waves (1-3 c.p.s.) occur more than 50 percent of the time. Slow-wave sleep has been correlated with numerous biochemical changes that are associated with healing and rejuvenation of the body.

subdominant hemispheric functioning in most right-handed people the left hemisphere is dominant (verbal, linear functioning), and the right hemisphere (non-verbal, holistic functioning) is sub-dominant. Subdominant hemispheric functioning is characterized by increased brain-wave frequency, associated with non-verbal and holistic functioning. While the left/right brain model is still widely used in science, the latest research suggests that there is far more redundancy between the two hemispheres than was previously thought.

tantric dream yoga (see "dream yoga" and "Dzogchen Practice of the Clear Light") tantra is connected to the Sanskrit root meaning "to weave." Indian and Tibetan tantra is a series of texts that detail yogic methods to rapidly accelerate one's evolution towards enlightenment. Tantric dream yoga is creating "union" (yoga) with the source, or attaining enlightenment through dreams.

transcendence a state of consciousness wherein one rises above, moves beyond, or pierces, consensual reality. Transcendence occurs when one breaks through the maya, the illusion of the material world, and directly experiences ALL THAT IS (the implicate order)/

ultradian rhythms "Ultradian" literally means "more often than a day". Discovered by Nathaniel Kleitman and Eugene Aserinski, they are the internal biological rhythms which repeat approximately sixteen times per day, every 90-100 minutes. During sleeping hours, the ultradian rhythm parallels the non-REM/REM sleep cycle.

unconscious mind (see "conscious mind", "higher conscious mind") the aspect of oneself which is outside the conscious awareness. It is metaphorically referred to as the "storehouse" of all memories, emotions, and automatic functions. Learning, memory, motivation, and drives, as well as autonomic nervous system functions such as breathing, circulation, digestion, endocrine regulation and immune response, are all examples of some of these automatic functions. The unconscious mind contrasts with the conscious mind, which is one's present awareness.

void (see "implicate order," "frequency domain") Buddhist term for the unmanifest manifest; the unknown known, the implicate order in Bohm's theory from which all matter is created. The place of creation, a deeper level of reality where all things exist as possibilities and a place which cannot be known through the senses. Often referred to as the "One without a second."

wave (see "particle") a disturbance moving through some type of medium, e.g., a wave moving across water. A quantum "object" can appear as either a wave or particle. When it acts as wave it spreads throughout space. When it behaves as a particle it occupies only one point of space at a time. In scientific observation it is one or the other. The concept that matter can exist as either a wave or a particle but cannot be observed as both simultaneously is known as wave-particle duality.

witness consciousness, witness vision, witness position	a state of conscious dissociation where the position of one's awareness is outside the body, allowing for the detached observation of one's actions; being a witness to one's own actions.
Yogavasistha	a sacred Hindu text which explains how the act of dreaming (or emitting images) in human beings is an opportunity to experience the Divine nature of creation, which is usually thoughts to only be experienced by the god(s).

Index

Bibliography

Assagioli, Roberto, *The Act Of Will*, Penguin Books, New York, NY, USA, 1974

Bell, John Stuart, "On the Einstein, Podolsky, Rosen paradox", *Physics (1)*, 1964

Bernheim, H, *Suggestive Therapeutics: A Treatise On The Nature And Uses Of Hypnotism*, Putnam, New York, NY, USA, 1886

Bohm, David, *Wholeness And The Implicate Order*, Routledge & Kegan Paul, Boston, MA, USA, 1980

Brown, Peter, *The Hypnotic Brain*, Yale University Press, New Haven, CT, USA, 1991

Capra, Fritjof, *The Tao Of Physics*, Shambala, Boston, MA, USA, 1975

Capra, Fritjof, *Uncommon Wisdom*, Simon and Schuster, New York, NY, USA, 1988

Castaneda, Carlos, *The Art Of Dreaming*, HarperCollins, New York, NY, USA, 1993

Castaneda, Carlos, *The Eagle's Gift*, Simon and Schuster, New York, NY, USA, 1981

Casteneda, Carlos, *The Fire From Within*, Simon & Schuster, New York, NY, USA, 1984

Castaneda, Carlos, *Journey To Ixtlan*, Simon and Schuster, New York, NY, USA, 1972

Casteneda, Carlos, *The Power Of Silence*, Simon & Schuster, New York, NY, USA, 1987

Castaneda, Carlos, *Tales Of Power*, Simon and Schuster, New York, NY, USA, 1974

Chopra, Deepak, *Sacred Verses, Healing Sounds Volume I* (audiotapes), New World Library, San Rafael, CA, USA, 1994

Cochran, Tracy & Zaleski, Jeff, *Transformations*, Bell Tower Books, New York, NY, USA, 1995

DeLozier, Judith & Grinder, John, *Turtles All The Way Down: Prerequisites To Personal Growth*, Grinder, DeLozier and Associates, Bonny Doon, CA, USA, 1987

Desai, Amrit, *In The Presence Of A Master* (edited by Christine Deslauriers), Kripalu Yoga Fellowship, Lenox, MA, USA, 1992

Donner, Florinda, *Being-In-Dreaming*, HarperSanFrancisco, CA, USA, 1991

Dossey, Larry, *Healing Words*, HarperCollins, San Francisco, CA, USA, 1993

Friedman, Norman, *Bridging Science And Spirit*, Living Lake Books, St. Louis, MS, USA, 1990

Gackenbach, Jayne & Bosweld, Jane, *Control Your Dreams*, HarperPerennial, New York, NY, USA, 1988

Garfield, Patricia, *Creative Dreaming*, Ballantine Books, New York, NY, USA, 1974

Goldberg, Natalie, *Writing Down The Bones*, Shambala, Boston, MA, USA, 1986

Goodwin, Malcolm, *The Lucid Dreamer*, Simon and Schuster, New York, NY, USA, 1994

Green, Celia & McCreery, Charles, *Lucid Dreaming*, Routledge, London, UK, 1994

Herbert, Nick, *Quantum Reality*, Doubleday, New York, NY, USA, 1985

Hobson, J Allan, *The Chemistry Of Conscious States,* Little, Brown and Co., Boston, MA, USA, 1994

Hobson, J Allan, *The Dreaming Brain,* HarperCollins, New York, USA, 1988

Hobson, J Allan, *Sleep,* Scientific American Library, New York, NY, USA, 1989

Hobson, J Allan & McCarley, RW, "The brain as a dream state generator: an activation-synthesis hypothesis of the dream process," *American Journal Of Psychiatry 134* (12), 1977

James, Tad & Flynn, Ardie, *Lost Secrets Of Ancient Hawaiian Huna, Prepublication Manuscript,* Advanced Neuro Dynamics, Honolulu, HI, USA, 1993

Korzybski, Alfred, *Science And Sanity* (4th Edition), The International Non-Aristotelian Library, Lakeville, CT, USA, 1933

LaBerge, Stephen, "Dream re-entry as a way to lucid dreaming," *Night-Light: The Lucidity Institute Newsletter 3* (2), Spring 1991

LaBerge, Stephen, *Lucid Dreaming,* Ballantine Books, New York, NY, USA, 1985

LaBerge, Stephen & Rheingold, Howard, *Exploring The World Of Lucid Dreaming,* Ballantine Books, New York, NY, USA, 1990

LeCron, Leslie, "A hypnotic technique for uncovering unconscious material," *Journal Of Clinical Experimental Hypnosis 2,* 1954

Leichtman, Robert, *The Inner Side Of Life,* Ariel Press, Columbus, OH, USA, 1979

Maturano, Humberto & Varela, Francisco, *The Tree Of Knowledge: The Biological Roots Of Human Understanding,* Shambala, Boston, MA, USA, 1992

Norbu, Namkhai, *Dream Yoga And The Practice Of Natural Light*, edited by Michael Katz, Snow Lion Publications, Ithaca, NY, USA, 1992

Overdurf, John & Silverthorn, Julie, *Training Trances*, Metamorphous Press, Portland, OR, USA, 1995

Peat, F David, *Einstein's Moon: Bell's Theorem And The Curious Quest For Quantum Reality*, Contemporary Books, Chicago, IL, USA, 1990

Penfield, Wilder, *The Mystery Of The Mind: A Critical Study Of Consciousness And The Human Brain*, Princeton University Press, Princeton, NJ, USA, 1975

Pukui, Mary, Haertig, EW, & Lee, Catherine, *Nana I Ke Kumu, Volume I*, Hui Hanai, Honolulu, HI, USA, 1972

Pukui, Mary, Haertig, EW, & Lee, Catherine *Nana I Ke Kumu, Volume II*, Hui Hanai, Honolulu, HI, USA, 1972

Radha, Sivananda, *Realities Of The Dreaming Mind*, Timeless Books, Spokane, WA, USA, 1994

Rossi, Ernest, "Hypnosis and ultradian cycles: a new state(s) theory of hypnosis?" *American Journal Of Clinical Hypnosis 25*, 1982

Rossi, Ernest & Cheek, David, *Mind-Body Therapy*, W.W. Norton & Co., New York, NY, USA, 1988

Sandweiss, Samuel, *Sai Baba: The Holy Man...And The Psychiatrist*, Birth Day Publishing, San Diego, CA, USA, 1975

Sheldrake, Rupert, *Seven Experiments That Could Change The World*, Riverhead Books, New York, NY, USA, 1995

Talbot, Michael, *Mysticism And The New Physics*, Penguin Books, New York, NY, USA, 1981

Talbot, Michael, *The Holographic Universe*, HarperCollins, New York, NY, USA, 1991

Wheatley, Margaret, *Leadership And The New Science*, Berrett-Koehler Publishers, San Francisco, CA, USA, 1994

Wolf, Fred Alan, *The Dreaming Universe*, Simon & Schuster, New York, NY, USA, 1994

Wolf, Fred Alan, *Star Wave*, Macmillan, New York, NY, USA, 1984

Wolf, Fred Alan, *Taking The Quantum Leap*, HarperCollins, New York, NY, USA, 1989

Yogananda, Paramahansa, *The Autobiography Of A Yogi*, Self Realization Fellowship, Los Angeles, CA, USA, 1946

Training And Resources

Julie Silverthorn, M.S., and John Overdurf, C.A.C., offer a wide variety of training and resources for personal and professional development in the following areas:

Neuro-Linguisitc Programming and Human Neuro-Linguistic Psychology™

- Certified Practitioner of NLP and HNLP
- Certified Master Practitioner of NLP and HNLP
- Certified Trainer of NLP and HNLP
- Certified Master Trainer of NLP and HNLP

Hypnosis and Hypnotherapy Training

- Training Trances: Unconscious Healing And Beyond (Hypnosis II and III)
- Hypnosis Trainer's Training

Advanced Learning Seminars

- Trans-Learning™
- Spirit Of Creativity

For more information on audiotapes, books, videos, trainings, and other resources, please contact:

Neuro-Energetics
2137 Embassy Dirve
Suite 212
Lancaster, PA 17603 USA
717.293.8803 (home)
800.680.8803 (in USA)
717.293.0703 (fax)
enroll@nlptrainings.com (email)

Or visit us at: **www.nlptrainings.com**

For more information of the Dream Light™, Nova Dreamer™ and Dream Link™ contact:

The Lucidity Institute
Box 2364
Stanford
CA 94309
USA

Crown House Publishing Limited

Crown Buildings,
Bancyfelin,
Carmarthen, Wales, UK, SA33 5ND.
Telephone: +44 (0) 1267 211880
Facsimile: +44 (0) 1267 211882
e-mail: bshine@crownhouse.co.uk
Website: www.crownhouse.co.uk

The New Encyclopedia Of Stage Hypnotism
by Ormond McGill PhD — Hardback £29.99

Now It's YOUR Turn For Success! *Training And Motivational Techniques For Direct Sales And Multi-Level Marketing*
by Richard Houghton & Janet Kelly — Paperback £9.99

Peace Of Mind Is A Piece Of Cake
by Michael Mallows & Joseph Sinclair — Paperback £8.99

***The POWER Process**: An NLP Approach To Writing*
by Sid Jacobson & Dixie Elise Hickman — Paperback £12.99

Precision Therapy: *A Professional Manual Of Fast And Effective Hypnoanalysis Techniques*
by Duncan McColl PhD — Paperback £15.00

Rapid Cognitive Therapy: *The Professional Therapists' Guide To Rapid Change Work*
by Georges Philips & Terrence Watts — Hardback £20.00

Scripts & Strategies In Hypnotherapy
by Roger P. Allen — Hardback £19.99

The Secrets Of Magic: *Communicational Excellence For The 21st Century*
by L. Michael Hall PhD — Paperback £12.99

***Seeing The Unseen**: A Past Life Revealed Through Hypnotic Regression*
by Ormond McGill PhD — Paperback £12.99

Slimming With Pete: *Taking The Weight Off Body AND Mind*
by Pete Cohen & Judith Verity — Paperback £9.99

Smoke-Free And No Buts!
byDr Geoff Ibbotson & Dr Ann Williamson — Paperback £5.99

***Solution States**: A Course In Solving Problems In Business With The Power Of NLP*
by Sid Jacobson — Paperback £12.99

***The Spirit Of NLP**: The Process, Meaning And Criteria For Mastering NLP*
by L. Michael Hall PhD — Paperback £12.99

***The Sourcebook Of Magic**: A Comprehensive Guide To NLP Techniques*
by L. Michael Hall PhD & Barbara Belnap — Paperback £14.99

Sporting Excellence: *Optimising Sports Performance Using NLP*
by Ted Garratt — Paperback £9.99

***Time-Lining**: Patterns For Adventuring In "Time"*
by Bob G. Bodenhamer DMin & L. Michael Hall PhD — Paperback £14.99

The User's Manual For The Brain: *The Complete Manual For Neuro-Linguistic Programming Practitioner Certification*
by Bob G. Bodenhamer DMin & L. Michael Hall PhD — A4 binder £30.00

***Vibrations For Health And Happiness**: Everyone's Easy Guide To Stress-free Living*
by Tom Bolton — Paperback £9.99

Order form

**********Special offer: 4 for the price of 3!!!**********

Buy 3 books & we'll give you a 4th title - FREE!

(free title will be book of lowest value)

Qty	*Title*
—	*Change Management Excellence*
—	*Doing It With Pete*
—	*Dreaming Realities*
—	*Ericksonian Approaches*
—	*Figuring Out People*
—	*Gold Counselling® Second Edition*
—	*Grieve No More, Beloved*
—	*Hypnotherapy Training In The UK*
—	*Influencing With Integrity*
—	*Instant Relaxation*
—	*The Magic Of Mind Power*
—	*A Multiple Intelligences Road To An ELT Classroom*
—	*Multiple Intelligences Poster Set*
—	*New Encyclopedia Of Stage Hypnotism*
—	*Now It's YOUR Turn For Success!*
—	*Peace Of Mind Is A Piece Of Cake*
—	*The POWER Process*
—	*Precision Therapy*
—	*Rapid Cognitive Therapy*
—	*Scripts & Strategies In Hypnotherapy*
—	*The Secrets Of Magic*
—	*Seeing The Unseen*
—	*Slimming With Pete*
—	*Smoke-Free And No Buts!*
—	*Solution States*
—	*The Sourcebook Of Magic*
—	*The Spirit Of NLP*
—	*Sporting Excellence*
—	*Time-Lining*
—	*The User's Manual For The Brain*
—	*Vibrations For Health And Happiness*

Postage and packing

UK:	*£2.50 for one book*
	£4.50 for two or more books
Europe:	*£3.50 per book*
Rest of the world	*£4.50 per book*

My details:

Name: Mr/Mrs/Ms/Other (please specify) ....

Address: ....

....

....

Postcode: ....*Daytime tel:* ....

I wish to pay by:

❏ *Amex* ❏ *Visa* ❏ *Mastercard* ❏ *Switch – Issue no./Start date:* ....

Card number:...*Expiry date:*...

Name on card:..*Signature:*..

❏ *cheque/postal order payable to* ***AA Books***

Please send me the following catalogues:

- ❏ *Accelerated Learning (Teaching Resources)*
- ❏ *Accelerated Learning (Personal Growth)*
- ❏ *Neuro-Linguistic Programming*
- ❏ *NLP Video Library – hire (UK only)*
- ❏ *NLP Video Library – sales*
- ❏ *Ericksonian Hypnotherapy*
- ❏ *Classical Hypnosis*
- ❏ *Gestalt Therapy*
- ❏ *Psychotherapy/Counselling*
- ❏ *Employment Development*
- ❏ *Business*
- ❏ *Freud*
- ❏ *Jung*
- ❏ *Transactional Analysis*
- ❏ *Parenting*
- ❏ *Special Needs*

Please fax/send to:

The Anglo American Book Company,
FREEPOST SS1340
Crown Buildings, Bancyfelin,
Carmarthen, West Wales,
United Kingdom, SA33 4ZZ,
Tel: +44 (0) 1267 211880/211886 Fax: +44 (0) 1267 211882
or e-mail your order to:
books@anglo-american.co.uk